Foundations of
Behavioral Science Research
in Organizations

Behavioral Science in Industry Series

Edited by Victor H. Vroom
Yale University

□ = //

Foundations of Behavioral Science Research in Organizations

Sheldon Zedeck
University of California, Berkeley

Milton R. Blood
Georgia Institute of Technology

Brooks/Cole Publishing Company
Monterey, California
A Division of Wadsworth Publishing Company, Inc.

To the Mother Superior of
industrial/organizational psychology (P. C. S.);
and to M. A. Z. and J. B.

ISBN: 0-8185-0116-2
L.C. Catalog Card No.: 73-89594
Printed in the United States of America
2 3 4 5 6 7 8 9 10—78 77 76 75

Illustrations: Creative Repro Photolithographers, Monterey, California
Typesetting: Continental Data Graphics, Culver City, California
Printing & Binding: Malloy Lithographing, Inc., Ann Arbor, Michigan

preface

Foundations of Behavioral Science Research in Organizations is a methods-oriented introduction to the field of industrial and organizational psychology organized around the major problems that must be dealt with when developing and maintaining an organization. The book is intended for use as an introductory text for undergraduates and as an outline for a detailed examination of the field at the graduate level. It is appropriate for use as a core text with paperbound volumes from the Behavioral Science in Industry Series or as a supplement to more traditional industrial psychology texts. In either case, it can be read by students in psychology, business administration, industrial engineering, public health, and other disciplines. It may also be useful to managers, personnel directors, applied psychologists, researchers, practitioners, and others who are already involved in some area of industrial/organizational psychology because it shows new ways to analyze and approach problems encountered in the work setting. The book is more easily understood if the reader has some elementary knowledge of statistics.

In contrast to most traditional books in the field, this book does not review the great mass of research literature. Instead, problems encountered in the work setting are examined, and ways of dealing with these problems are suggested and reviewed. This book's premise is that results do not readily generalize, whereas methods, procedures, and data-analysis techniques do. For each major problem, discussion includes implications of the problem area for the total organization, examination of the kinds of information necessary to understand and deal with the problem, and the techniques available for obtaining the appropriate information in order to solve or correct the problem. The chapters follow the logical sequence of *developing* the organization, *selecting* members to work in it, and, finally, *maintaining* the total organization.

The chapters should be studied sequentially since each one is based on the information in preceding chapters. Chapter One explores the value of theory, discusses whether results can be generalized, compares laboratory and field research, and develops a hypothetical organization that will illustrate certain points in subsequent chapters. In the rest of the book, we identify problems of organizations and present methods that can be applied to solve them, regardless of their individual variation.

Section I (Chapters Two and Three) concerns developing an organization; it discusses organizational characteristics, decision making, job analysis, and job design. Section II (Chapters Four, Five, and Six) deals with selecting members for the organization and the problems of criterion development, performance assessments, and training. Finally, Section III (Chapters Seven and Eight) is about maintaining the organization once the members have been selected; this section examines reward systems and assessment of member attitudes.

Much of the literature in industrial/organizational psychology concerns the application of research results to a particular method or situation. We urge the reader to supplement his use of this book by reading some of the works listed in the references at the end of each chapter. The text can then serve as the critical framework for evaluating the literature.

We would like to acknowledge the help of the following reviewers: Robert Andrews, Simon Frazer University; C. J. Bartlett, University of Maryland; Larry L. Cummings, University of Wisconsin; Charles L. Hulin, University of Illinois; Nick Imparato, University of San Francisco; William McGehee, Fieldcrest Mills; Stanley M. Nealey, Colorado State University; Albert Polin, University of Southern California; Kenneth Pool, Eastern Michigan University; Patricia C. Smith, Bowling Green State University; and Victor H. Vroom, Yale University. We would also like to thank typists Penelope Adams, Deedra McClearn, and Irene M. Vanderpool.

Sheldon Zedeck
Milton R. Blood

contents

chapter
one
Introduction

This book is built around the problems that arise when people work. Some of the problems lie with the individual and some with the organizations within which they work. Our interest is in the contributions which behavioral scientists can make toward the solutions of work-related problems. For example, how can we match the design of machines to the abilities of people? How can we evaluate a worker's contribution to the effectiveness of an organization? On what basis can we choose workers when there are more applicants than available positions? On what basis does an organization reward workers?

Work is the use of one's faculties to accomplish a goal. Like beauty, work may be in the eyes of the beholder—that is, a phenomenological rather than a logical term. Raising roses may be work for a gardener but recreation for an electrician. We do not want to define *work* as that which a person does to earn a living since that would exclude a great deal of work done by volunteers and dollar-a-year government executives. We would find general agreement that Alan Shepard was "working" as an astronaut when he went to the moon even though he was a millionaire and need not have gone to the moon to earn his living.

As most work is done in organizations or through the combined efforts of several people, we will be concerned not only with individual behavior but also with interactions among workers and with activities and structures which are developed to coordinate work behavior among several persons. Individuals form organizations to accomplish objectives. These organizations are often divided into small, interdependent subgroups. Thus, we will consider the interrelationships among people, subgroups, and the organization.

Human behavior at work is certainly as complex as human behavior in other settings. Therefore, we will not proceed through "the five simple keys" or "the seven golden rules" of understanding work behavior. In fact, one of the principal tenets of this book is that there are very few "general" statements about human behavior that will be useful in solving specific problems. The complexities of human behavior, then, necessitate an understanding of multiple variables and contingencies, and *we are not likely to find the answers to specific situations in our knowledge of general cases.* People differ from each other in many ways, and they change from time to time. It would be short-sighted of us to expect that human behavior could be predicted and understood as accurately as the "behavior" of a chemical compound. If six test tubes of the same chemical are treated the same, they will respond the same; if six people are treated the same, they may all respond differently. In fact, if one individual receives the same treatment six times, he might respond differently each time.

Organizations are as complex as the individuals within them. Organizations may be small or large, production- or service-oriented, profit-making or nonprofit-making (intentionally or unintentionally), rigid or flexible, and so on. The ways in which organizations differ are as numerous as the ways in which people differ. This, as we will see later in the book, poses problems when one attempts to gain scientific information about organizations.

The complexities of workers and work organizations do not mean that no generalizations are possible. They do, however, indicate that predictions (every decision to take an action is a prediction) about a particular worker, a particular work situation, or a particular work organization should be made with a great deal of caution. The specific instance for which the prediction is made may not fit the generalization on which the prediction is based. Therefore, *as much information as possible should be collected from the specific instance about which a decision is to be made.* This is our basic thesis.

Why Study Work and Work Organizations?

Any modern society depends on the work which is done by its members. That work must be coordinated; the workers must somehow be motivated; and the society will prosper in relation to the efficiency of the task accomplishment. In an industrial society the most important resource is the people. The society exists for the people and the work is done by them. Even in economic terms labor is the most valuable resource of almost all industrial organizations. (Most car repair bills, for example, include a larger cost for labor than for parts.) But, of course, the importance of the members of an industrial society transcends their economic value. In a more fundamental sense the people are the society. Because they are the essence of the society, there can be no more important part.

Behavioral scientists study the work behaviors of people, first of all, because they are curious. Work behavior is a substantial part of the lives of many workers, and many behavioral scientists are trying to increase their understanding of this important phenomenon. Additionally, society encourages behavioral scientists to study work behavior because the results may suggest ways to make work more pleasant or better suited to human physical and psychological capacities, to coordinate work activities, and to match persons and tasks more appropriately. This book will be built around some of the problems which behavioral scientists can help solve.

Importance of Methodology

To behavioral scientists, one of the most troublesome consequences of the fact that work is usually done in organizations that differ is that the results of studies conducted within one organization rarely generalize to other organizations. What we find in a study of the communications among the members of the United States Senate may be very unlike the communications in the Ford Motor Company or in Hooper, Grant, Clark, and Horowitz, Attorneys at Law. The work goals of refrigerator assemblers may differ from those of the Radio City Rockettes. In fact, the characteristics which lead to success as a real estate salesman in one company may differ from those which promote success as a salesman in the realty company next door.

This perplexing state of affairs could be alleviated by finding ways of describing the similarities and differences among work organizations. We could describe organizations on the basis of their size, technology, assets, style of leadership, procedure for decision making, and many other characteristics. If these characteristics could then be related to the results of studies carried out in these organizations, it would be possible to generalize results from one organization to another. The catch in such a plan is determining the relevant ways of describing an organization. An example of this problem is the variety of results obtained in studies of the relationship between worker satisfaction and performance. Different studies have found that high satisfaction accompanies high performance, that high satisfaction accompanies low performance, or that there is no relationship between satisfaction and performance.

If we could identify the relevant characteristics of the organizations in which these different results were found, we could generalize from one organization to another. Unfortunately, we have not often been able to identify and/or measure the variables relevant to these organizations. Knowledge gained from the field of psychology is much better suited to understanding individuals. It is only recently that researchers have focused on organizations and organizational behavior.

If we want to understand individuals, we collect a large sample of individuals and measure the behavior in question. If we want to describe intelligence, we develop measures of intelligence on a representative sample of thousands (or at least hundreds) of people. Similarly, if we want to describe the dimension of leadership style of organizations in general, we must get a large sample of organizations on which to develop our measurement instrument. Yet, with few exceptions, studies of organizations have been carried out in one, two, or possibly as many as six organizations. We would scoff at a researcher who suggested that he understood intelligence from a study of six people, and we should be equally skeptical that we can understand an organization's characteristics by studying data from only a few of them.

This inability to identify and measure the relevant variables makes it difficult to assess the degree of similarity and difference among organizations. Given that the organizational context is an important determinant of our research results, this uniqueness should make us very wary of generalizations of results from one organization to another. That is, organizations may be similar or different along any number of salient dimensions. We cannot use this information, however, until we can make adequate studies to determine *which* dimensions are influential in *what* situations and *how* those dimensions can be measured. There is no indication that we are approaching such knowledge, and in most cases we will be more effective if we treat research results as unique to the organization in which the research was done.

On the other hand, the information-gathering techniques which we use in different organizations often are generalizable. Although we may expect different results, the methods used to study communications in different organizations will often be the same. If you are interested in selecting managers for your organization, you would not want to use the results of management selection research done in another organization, but you will probably gain by considering how they did their research. In the complex world of work organizations, methods for information gathering generalize much more than *results* of information gathering. Consequently, when attempting to solve the problems of an organization, it is better to know how to seek information than to know what information has been found elsewhere. However, the results of information gathering in other organizations provide insights or starting points for the investigation in your specific situation.

The focus of this book is the techniques and strategies by which information about workers is sought. That is not to say that there is *no* general information about workers and work organizations; where such information is available it will be presented. Nonetheless, the reader is encouraged to be skeptical about believing that results presented here are necessarily applicable to specific problems of which he is aware.

Strategies of Information Collecting

There are many kinds of information available on worker-related problems. Although we insist that it is best to use scientific information whenever possible, much of the information concerning the problems discussed in this book derives from practice rather than scientific investigation. Because a wealth of "how to" books based on "my experience as a successful managerial genius" suggest solutions for the problems raised in this book, some effort will be made to characterize the differences between information obtained from practice and information gathered scientifically. "Practice" and "science," then, are data-gathering methods, and we will consider both methods as ways of getting information about the solution of a specific problem in a work organization.

One of the most important differences is that the scientific method is always concerned with multiple events whereas practice often attempts to extract usable information from single examples. The problem with the practice approach is summed up in a Yiddish proverb: " 'For example' is not proof." We can be easily misled by a single or a few examples because we may attend to inappropriate aspects of the situation. If we watched only the masters golf tournament we might conclude (erroneously) that the best golfers are left handed, and we might encourage potential employers of golfers to hire only left-handed persons. The scientific method, on the other hand, involves observations of multiple events and attempts to discover the variables common to all of them. If we watch several golf tournaments we may decide that the common characteristic among the winners is not right or left handedness but breadth of shoulders, ability to concentrate, and so on.

A second difference between the scientific method and practice pertains to the number of characteristics studied. In the scientific method, many characteristics are studied and each can take on different values. The same characteristics are examined for each of several events. In the case of practice, these characteristics, or variables, are infinite. Even when multiple events are studied, different variables may be examined in each event. Although common sense may rule out some variables, many must be considered. As noted above, there is a danger of attributing effects to the wrong variable and/or overlooking the appropriate variable. Also, there will be many variables about which the investigator will be uncertain. The color of a golfer's shoes is probably inconsequential, but what about the number of spikes? The strength of a golfer is surely an important consideration, but is a golfer's weight important?

To answer these questions, the scientific method attempts to observe (measure) all of the potentially influential variables. Depending on the particular strategy the investigator decides to use, he may control the variations in these characteristics statistically or by experimental manipulation. Experimental manipulation could involve the use of control groups, whereas statistical control could be achieved by statistical analyses such as various regression techniques. In any event, when the investigator is finished he will have observed a fairly limited set of variables and he will be able to make quantitative statements about the degree to which they are related. In this way he can find out if he has ignored the important variables. If he has, he will have statistical information that the observed variables have little effect on each other. Although we may discover that the variables which we investigated were not relevant, we may not be able to determine which variables *are* relevant.

Of course, it is not just the number of events or variables observed that differentiates the practitioner and the scientist. A person may observe many golf matches and pay attention to a few select variables yet have no scientific information. Scientific data must be systematically collected. Usually the data are quantified in some way so that they can be systematically analyzed. Systematic and specifiable data collection and analysis is absolutely essential to the scientific method and is one of its major virtues. Scientific data collection can be replicated; that is, conclusions can be tested by repeating the data collection techniques on a second (or third or fourth) set of data. But what can we do with the data based on examples? We can simply think of supportive or contradictory examples about which we have no more certainty than we had with the original. (If we begin to collect multiple examples *systematically*, we are making a scientific data collection and the point is moot.) However, the examples on which the first conclusions were based cannot be repeated. In this circumstance, perhaps the best procedure is a scientific examination of the conclusions drawn from practice.

A final crucial difference between the two methods is the trust we can put in our conclusions. Conclusions based on experience or practice are of unknown risk. That is, we know that they may be false, but we don't know how likely that possibility is. With systematic data collection and analysis we explicitly state the statistical probability that our conclusions are false. Statistical data analyses permit us to determine whether the results are due to chance. If specific results are likely to occur by chance less than 1 time in 20, we conclude that the resulting relationships are reliable. That is, the same relationship would be consistent in repetitions of the research. Statistical analyses help us eliminate from consideration those variables which are unrelated to the phenomenon we are interested in and, thus, our information search can be made more efficiently. We can come to correct conclusions based on experience, but we have no way of *knowing* whether we have done so or what the risk is that we have not. The value of information gathered through practice is that it generates hypotheses that should be investigated by the scientific method.

Scientific Method

There are three essential components of the scientific method. As they are all interdependent and all essential, there is no way of specifying their priority. One of the essentials—scientific theory— organizes the observations that have been made and provides a structure for the use of information obtained. Although the observations (data) are not open to manipulation by the scientist,* the organization of those observations is manipulable. Usually scientists can agree on what the observations are. Most scientific debates are over alternate ways of organizing observations. If two alternative models make equally adequate accounts of the available data, scientists will usually choose the one which is more parsimonious (requires fewer assumptions). Other considerations which are sometimes used in selecting among competing theories are (1) the purpose of the person who wants to use the information in the observations, and (2) the personal taste of the investigator.

Notice that we have not mentioned anything about the closeness of our theory to *truth*. That is because the scientific enterprise has no way of knowing whether or not its theories approach that mystical concept. Early medical researchers were as convinced that blood did not circulate throughout the body as later researchers are that it does. Later researchers supported their circulation theory with observations which had not been available to their predecessors and which could not be explained by a noncirculation theory. Our current theories of blood flow explain more observations than did earlier notions. But can we be sure that presently unknown observation techniques will not require us to reorganize our conceptions about the processes of body fluids? Of course not. Even those scientific theories which we question least are limited by the observational techniques available to us, and new methods of observation may force us to restructure our theories.

Scientific theories specify (1) the salient characteristics of the objects being studied and (2) the relationships among those characteristics. The characteristics are called *theoretical units*, and the relationships are called *laws of interaction*. Scientific investigators often do not define the theoretical units and laws of interaction in their research, but some theory is implicit in almost all data

*The reader can object that data reports are certainly manipulable. However, it is perhaps the world's largest conspiratorial gentlemen's agreement that scientists report their data accurately and accept as accurate the data reports of other scientists.

collection and analysis. If there is no theory, then there is no science in the full sense. The mere collection of observations (for example, the census) without some attempt at understanding and organizing the observations and the relations among them is not science.

The second essential of the scientific method is the establishment of *empirical indicators* for the units of the theory. The empirical indicator is the technique or operation which the investigator uses to measure the values on the theoretical units. It is important that the units under investigation have specifiable measurement techniques. They must be specified so that they can be replicated by others, and so that others will know precisely how the values for the theoretical units were derived. Suppose we were investigating a theoretical statement such as:

Sales ability   is positively related to   friendliness.

      unit   law of interaction   unit

For the theoretical unit "sales ability" one empirical indicator could be the dollar value of goods sold in a month. Of course, other empirical indicators might be chosen for "sales ability"—number of sales, frequency of exchanges, or number of customer complaints. Likewise, we can have several empirical indicators for the theoretical unit of "friendliness"—ratings by fellow salespersons, ratings by customers, or number of times the salesperson is specifically requested by customers. The choice of an empirical indicator may influence the results obtained, and many seeming contradictions in scientific research result from the use of different empirical indicators for the same theoretical unit.

If we want scientific information about the theoretical statement, we must specify the empirical indicators for each theoretical unit and measure many salespersons. Scientifically, we cannot accept the statement on the grounds that it seems true intuitively or on the basis of having known a very good salesperson who was friendly. Much of this book will be concerned with finding or constructing adequate empirical indicators for the theoretical units with which we are concerned in problem-solving investigations.

The third essential of the scientific method is analysis of the data. The empirical indicators allow us to obtain values for the theoretical units, and the data analyses test the laws of interaction in the theory. Social science data analyses usually are statistical. This is very important since statistical analyses provide indications of the confidence an investigator can have in his results. According to probability theory, if a result could occur *by chance* less than 1 time in 20 then we generally feel that we can have confidence in our results. (This frequency is generally accepted but is not a hard and fast rule to be applied in all situations.) Stated another way, if the result could occur *by chance* more often than 1 time in 20, we take a greater risk in accepting our results as a confirmation of the tested law of interaction. This book should help the reader understand what statistical techniques are appropriate to various situations and will point out some of the limitations of various statistical methods. However, the reader is encouraged to supplement this information by developing a knowledge of statistical analysis (see data analysis references). Without the analysis of empirical data, theories are not scientific. Theories are merely opinions or possibilities of unknown certainty until confirmed by analyses.

A Comparison of Laboratory and Field Studies

Throughout this book we will be examining problems and procedures that relate to industrial and organizational psychology. Possible solutions to these problems are usually investigated or tested in the laboratory or in the field or natural environment. Consequently, the test situation can be either simulated and controlled or naturally occurring events which are amenable to investigation. Several interdependent factors must be considered when choosing a setting:

1. *Problem under investigation.* Specific problems that surface in the field can be studied in the field or laboratory. Though problems are identified in the field, investigations of general theories of work behavior are more suited to initial investigation in the laboratory. Laboratory experiments are appropriate for systematically assessing and identifying important and irrelevant variables. Once the theory is developed, it can be examined in the field.

Suppose that many people are quitting shortly after joining an organization. Research into the causes of the high quitting rate could be conducted in the field. The organization might institute certain policy changes and then observe the effect of the changes on the rate. Or the organization might administer a questionnaire to assess employee reasons for quitting. On the other hand, the same problem can be studied in a laboratory setting. Laboratory situations could be systematically varied to discover what characteristics lead people to leave the situation. The characteristics to be investigated would be chosen according to what the investigators believe are relevant or on the basis of previous research on the problem of quitting. The point is, though, that results from the laboratory should not be applied in the specific situation with the assumption that they will be effective. This assumption must be tested, systematically.

2. *Participants in research projects.* Motivation of participants is a problem in research. In a laboratory study, the participants are either volunteers, fulfilling a requirement for an introductory psychology course, or paid for their efforts. In any case, the researcher must rely on their motivation and willingness for cooperation (in fact, cooperation can be excessive, resulting in the participants' attempts to determine and then fulfill the researcher's hypotheses). In the field study, a frequent procedure is to inform the participants that the results "won't affect you" and then hope that the participants become as involved as if the results *would* affect them.

Related to the problem of motivation is the degree of involvement of the researcher. The presence of the researcher is usually obvious in a laboratory and again, may affect the responses of the participants. In the field, however, the researcher may be an uninvolved observer. He can obtain measures so discreetly that the participants do not realize that their inputs will be used in data analysis. This type of measurement, in which the measurement process does not influence the measured values, is called *unobtrusive,* or *nonreactive.* For example, if we wanted to assess the esteem in which an employee is held by an organization, we could unobtrusively observe such measures as size of the office, number of windows, whether there is a view, year and make of the company car, and so on.

Finally, the researcher will often have the problem of obtaining management's permission to conduct a study. If he does, to facilitate cooperation, the researcher often will have to convince the participants that he is not management's tool. Accomplishing the latter may conflict with the former.

3. *Sample size and representativeness.* The size of the sample used in an investigation often will influence the choice of a research site. From a physical standpoint it is difficult to examine a problem in a laboratory setting if the sample size needed to represent the group to which the results would be applicable is too large. Another factor to be considered is the representativeness of the sample. The sample should be representative of the group to whom you're to generalize. If it is the actual sample in the organization there is obviously little problem, but if it is a laboratory situation, one must take care that the sample is representative.

4. *Variables investigated.* The number and type of independent and dependent variables (theoretical units) examined is important when deciding whether to conduct field or laboratory research. Independent variables are selected or changed by the researcher to determine their influence on other variables. Dependent variables are affected by the independent variables. Often the independent variables are not replicated well enough or strongly enough in the laboratory, thereby diminishing any effects. In the field, however, events usually occur naturally and the variables operate at their real strength. The laboratory is sometimes used to exaggerate variables that occur only sporadically or rarely occur at full strength in the field. In field research, however, the researcher has the problem of waiting for the event to occur or of deciding when in the cycle of events to begin his observation.

Related to both types of variables is the problem of interaction. Interactions occur when the joint effect of two or more independent variables is different from their separate effects. For example, level of satisfaction and years of experience (considered as independent variables) may be related to productivity (a dependent variable) in such a manner that satisfaction is not related to production except among experienced workers. Suppose we find the weekly production records (shown in Figure 1.1) for employees divided into groups on the basis of level of satisfaction and years of experience. An examination of the figure shows that at the low satisfaction level the amount of experience does not influence performance. Similarly, at the low experience level satisfaction does not influence performance. The combination of high satisfaction and long experience, however, results in a performance level much greater than the other combinations.

EXPERIENCE	less than 5 years	150	150
	more than 5 years	150	250
		low satisfaction	high satisfaction

SATISFACTION

FIGURE 1.1. *Weekly units of production.*

The conclusion is that the variables of experience and satisfaction *interact* in their influence on performance.

A consequence of examining a large number of variables is the increased chance that results will indicate that many of the variables are jointly affecting the dependent variable, which makes interpretation and understanding of the processes involved more complex. The practical contribution of an effect is not often greatly increased when one variable is added to a large set of variables. A laboratory examination would indicate which variables do not influence others to a large degree, either alone or jointly, and thus can be eliminated in a field test of the results. Elimination of unnecessary variables conserves time, effort, and money.

5. *Control.* Researchers can be misled if the results are influenced by factors or characteristics other than those in which the researcher is interested. The results of a study conducted to examine the relationship between the experience and the productivity of employees may be influenced by the fact that more experienced employees are also older. In this case, age is a *confounding* or *contaminating* variable for the variable of experience. Confounding variables can be controlled statistically in both field and laboratory studies. Certain statistical procedures (partial correlations, analysis of covariance) are available for the purpose of examining the relationship between two variables of interest (experience and production) with the influence of a third variable (age) eliminated.

In addition, confounding variables can be controlled in a laboratory study by experimental design. For example, it would be relatively easy to obtain groups of subjects at different age levels in order to examine the relationship between experience and productivity in each age group. If experience is related to productivity, the same relationship should be found in all age groups. If the experience-productivity relationship is found in a research which does not control for age, the interpretation is limited by ignorance of the role age has played in the relationship. An important problem in social science research is determining potential confounding variables.

Control also implies that there is a control group which does not receive the experimental treatment. It is difficult to use a control group in the field, for management is often reluctant to administer a treatment or institute a change in only one part of the work force. If we are concerned with the effects of rest pauses on productivity in a laboratory situation one group of subjects could receive rest pauses (experimental group) and another group would not have rest pauses (control group). Then we would observe differences in productivity for the two groups. In a field study, rest pauses for part of a work force might cause conflict or be impractical because of the work technology.

A set of designs called *quasi-experimental designs* are appropriate for natural settings in which formal control groups are not available (Campbell & Stanley, 1963). These designs will be discussed where appropriate throughout the book.

6. *Realism vs. simulation.* Many work situations can be duplicated or simulated in the laboratory. The basic concerns are those of degree of simulation, effect of simulation, and cost. If duplication of the entire setting is not necessary and only the basic elements are needed, the laboratory can serve as a substitute for the real setting. An advantage to the laboratory setting is the reduction of interferences from extraneous factors in the work place. On the other hand, simulation itself can interact with the variables under investigation and yield results different from those that would be obtained in the natural setting. People may behave differently—for example, take more risks, work at a faster pace, and so on—because they realize they are not in an actual situation.

A limiting factor to simulation is cost of duplication for the organization and cost to the participant for leaving his setting. Also, an assumption frequently made of laboratory simulated research is that the results could be applied to a situation if the experimenter could determine that the general features of the situation have been simulated. This assumption is tenuous; such a notion ignores the specific effects of specific situations. Usually, methods are generalizable and results are not.

7. *Duration of research.* Long-term studies are possible in both the laboratory and natural settings. In the natural setting, the longer the research period, the more chance for confounding. Confounding can be due to change in personnel or personnel policy. Long-term research, however, permits the utilization and examination of natural changes. Short-term research, usually conducted in the laboratory, is appropriate when powerful change methods are available (see factor 4 above).

8. *Approach to change.* Another problem in research pertains to natural as opposed to purposeful change. As previously mentioned,

the field is ideal for studying natural change. The appropriate setting for purposeful change depends on what will be changed—the individual participants, general organizational policy, organizational structure, or organizational environment.

A related problem is massive versus controlled, gradual change. Whether the induced change is rapid or gradual depends on the amount of time allotted for experimentation, which is often determined by management and the cost involved. Also, in laboratory research the introduction of the treatment is similar to being on the job the first day whereas in field settings there is a more natural introductory process.

9. *Task.* Certain tasks are more suitable for laboratory than for field research and vice versa. However, in laboratory research, the given task receives all attention and emphasis, whereas in the field, the participants have additional duties and obligations. Hence, varying emphases can lead to different results and interpretations.

The basic advantage to field studies is realism. Field studies are most complete in the sense that they involve many more variables than laboratory studies (though many may be irrelevant). Laboratory studies are more efficient from a scientific viewpoint though the results they yield may be less complete and generalizable. Laboratory studies generally have less external validity (generalizability to other situations) and more internal validity (confidence that the obtained results can be attributed to the independent variables) than field studies. Consequently, the two approaches complement each other. The choice of one approach, if both are not possible, depends on the judged relative importance of realism, the degree of theory development, the desired precision of measurement, as well as cost and other practical or economic factors.

A General Industrial Situation

Throughout this book it will be helpful to refer to specific examples to demonstrate the problems which can occur when dealing with organizations of persons. Rather than creating an *ad hoc* example for every problem, we are introducing here a description of a generalized industrial organization. Explanations of later problems will be illustrated by how and where they would surface in this organization.

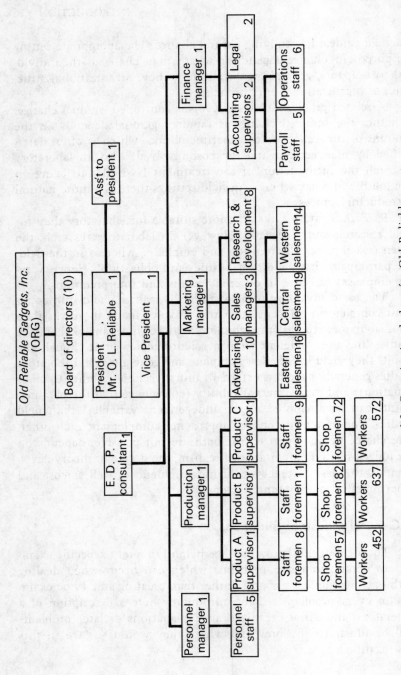

FIGURE 1.2. Organizational chart for Old Reliable Gadgets, Inc.

Figure 1.2 is an organizational chart of our generalized organization, Old Reliable Gadgets, Inc. (ORG), O. L. Reliable, President. The organizational chart shows the hierarchical relationships among the members of the organization and the number in each box indicates the number of organization members who perform their organizational duties in the role named in the box. How an organization's actual operations are related to the hypothetical arrangement displayed in this chart will be discussed as we discuss various aspects of the organization in later chapters. As you can see, the fundamental task of the organization is the production of three different gadgets: A, B, and C. Production is carried out by workers who are directed in their efforts by shop foremen. Staff foremen organize the efforts of multiple work crews, and for each gadget there is a product supervisor. A production manager is responsible for all production activities. Salesmen, whose activities are organized by three regional sales managers, market the gadgets. A marketing manager oversees the sales managers and two other functional units: advertising, and research and development.

Two groups in the organization contribute in a service role. That is, they are much less directly involved with the product. The personnel manager and his staff are concerned with many of the problems we will discuss in this book. They are responsible for staffing and training members throughout the organization. The finance manager and his staff are in charge of the organization's financial resources. Also reporting through the finance manager are two legal advisors. The electronic data processing consultant is available to all parts of the organization to help with electronic data processing (E.D.P.) problems and to inform workers of E.D.P. techniques which could help them perform their specific tasks. Executive tasks are handled by a three-person team: O. L. Reliable, the president; Harley Reliable, his son and vice president; and Bill Bufferin, the assistant to the president. Harley actually assists in the operation of the organization, whereas Bill usually works on special and *ad hoc* problems. A board of directors oversees the operation of the organization, but they will not enter into much of our discussion (O. L. is Chairman of the Board and the others are hand-picked abbetors). Excluding the Board of Directors, there are 2000 persons in ORG. But ORG is not presented as a typical organization (the authors would argue against the usefulness of "typical" cases). Service organizations, charitable institutions, and so on may have goals that differ from ORG, but similar organizational structures and problems are often encountered. Many of the problems discussed in the pages ahead could occur in ORG or any other organization, and we will refer to this model for illustrative purposes when it is appropriate.

The format of this book is based on one conception of the sequence in which problems arise in organizations. First, there are problems related to the *development* of the organizational structure and individual tasks in the organization. Second, once the structure is formalized, people must be *obtained* to staff the organization. Finally, the interaction between the structure and the people generates problems which must be dealt with to *maintain* the organization. Throughout the book, the reader should be aware of the interrelatedness of organizational problems.

References

Scientific Method

Dubin, R. *Theory building*. New York: Free Press, 1969.

Kaplan, A. *The conduct of inquiry*. Scranton, Pa.: Chandler, 1964.

McCain, G., & Segal, M. *The game of science*. Monterey, Calif.: Brooks/Cole, 1969.

Neale, J. M., & Liebert, R. M. *Science and behavior: An introduction to methods of research*. Englewood Cliffs, N. J.: Prentice-Hall, 1973.

Webb, E. J., Campbell, D. T., Schwartz, R. D., & Sechrest, L. *Unobtrusive measures: Nonreactive research in the social sciences*. Chicago: Rand McNally, 1966.

Laboratory or Field Research

Campbell, D. T., & Stanley, J. C. *Experimental and quasi-experimental designs for research*. Chicago: Rand McNally, 1963.

Festinger, L. Laboratory experiments. In L. Festinger and D. Katz (Eds.), *Research methods in the behavioral sciences*. New York: Holt, Rinehart & Winston, 1953. Pp. 136–172.

McGrath, J. E. Toward a "theory of method" for research on organizations. In W. W. Cooper, H. J. Leavitt, and M. W. Shelly (Eds.), *New perspectives in organization research*. New York: Wiley, 1964. Pp. 533–556.

Mechanic, D. Some considerations in the methodology of organizational studies. In H. J. Leavitt (Ed.), *The social science of organizations*. Englewood Cliffs, N. J.: Prentice-Hall, 1963. Pp. 137–182.

Orne, M. On the social psychology of the psychological experiment: With particular reference to demand characteristics and their implications. *American Psychologist*, 1962, **17,** 776–783.

Scott, W. R. Field methods in the study of organizations. In A. Etzioni (Ed.), *A sociological reader on complex organizations* (2nd ed.). New York: Holt, Rinehart & Winston, 1969. Pp. 558–576.

Seashore, S. E. Field experiments with formal organizations. *Human Organization*, 1964, **23,** 164–170.

Weick, K. E. Organizations in the laboratory. In V. H. Vroom (Ed.), *Methods of organizational research.* Pittsburgh: University of Pittsburgh Press, 1967. Pp. 1–56.

Weick, K. E. Laboratory experimentation with organizations. In J. G. March (Ed.), *Handbook of organizations.* Skokie, Ill.: Rand McNally, 1965. Pp. 194–260.

Zelditch, M., Jr. Can you really study an army in the laboratory? In A. Etzioni (Ed.), *A sociological reader on complex organizations* (2nd ed.). New York: Holt, Rinehart & Winston, 1969. Pp. 528–539.

Data Analysis

Hays, W. L. *Basic statistics.* Monterey, Calif.: Brooks/Cole, 1967.

Hays, W. L. *Statistics for the social scientists* (2nd ed.). New York: Holt, Rinehart & Winston, 1973.

McNemar, Q. *Psychological statistics* (4th ed.). New York: Wiley, 1969.

Developing the
Organization

chapter
two
Organizations

Most of what we know about organizations is based on the experiences of those who have been members of organizations and on the common sense that we have all gleaned from our own associations with organizations. Most of this "knowledge" has not been subjected to scientific examination or rigorous questioning. Intimate and extensive personal experiences with organizations have sometimes surfaced as "how to" books which have instructed the reader in the proper way to be an organizational member or leader. These writings are full of insightful assertions based on mostly untested hypotheses or theoretical statements about the operation of organizations. Because these assertions are untested, they may or may not be accurate in a general sense, and they are surely of unknown usefulness when we are faced with any specific organizational problem.

Perhaps we can gain some idea of why these insights have not been tested from a simple notion which was put forth in a popular book. In his delightful and insightful book *Up the Organization*, Robert Townsend asserts that "all decisions should be made as low as possible in the organization." That is a reasonable suggestion based on Townsend's first-hand organizational experience, but let us consider what would be necessary to test the utility of that statement in a scientific manner. First, we would need to restate the assertion in such a way that it is testable.

A variety of restatements are possible, and each of them has slightly different implications for our investigatory procedures: "Decisions made as low as possible in the organization are better than decisions made at other places in the organization," and "Organizations in which decisions are made as low as possible are better than organizations in which decisions are made elsewhere." The first of these statements is about decisions and the second is about organizations. Assuming that Townsend intended to say something which would be generalizable to many organizations, let us consider the problems of testing the second statement. Immediately we are faced with trying to specify the population of organizations to which we would like to generalize—all retail merchandizing organizations; all nonprofit organizations; all large organizations; all family-owned organizations; all possible organizations? Again, the problem is to determine the variables in the make-up of the population. The reason we must make this specification is so that we can carry out our investigation with either a representative or a random sample from the population. Once the population has been determined, a sample could be chosen so that the members of the sample have the same characteristics as the members of the population (representative sample) or so that every member of the population has an equal chance to be chosen as a member of the sample (random sample).

Next, we must find empirical indicators for the units of the theory. One of the units is a dimension or categorization scheme which would allow us to compare organizations and say which are better. That is, we must define in operational terms how we will measure the performance of organizations. Remember that we may have to make comparisons among organizations with different goals. Also, we need a way to differentiate organizations where decisions are made as low as possible from organizations where they are not. This implies not only that we have techniques for observing where decisions are made but also that we can discern whether an observed decision was made as low as possible. The crucial question is what is meant by "as low as possible." Only if we had a measure of organizational performance *and* an observation technique which differentiated organizations into low-decision and not-low-decision categories, *and* we carried out these measurements on a sample of organizations, could we test the restated assertion. Alternative restatements would require other tests. It is no wonder that much of what we know or want to know about organizations has not been rigorously researched.

Organizational Goals

One aspect which must be taken into account in almost any research about organizations is their goals. For what purposes do the organizations exist? This is often a very difficult question to answer even for a specific organization. Firms producing the same type of product may have different goals. One auto company may produce economical cars which will provide dependable transportation; another may produce luxury autos which will provide not only transportation but comfort and prestige. Differences in goals will probably necessitate some differences in organization. Secondary educational institutions may provide students with work skills, prepare them for college, or both. Again, their purpose is likely to dictate some specific organizational characteristics. To answer questions about the appropriate structure, size, technology, and so on, we will surely need to know the purpose of the organization. But that leads us to a problem: who defines the organizational purpose?

There are several potential sources for a definitive statement of organizational purpose. One is, of course, the titular head of the policy-making part of the organization—the chairman of the board of ORG, the president of the P.T.A., or the publisher of a newspaper. The members of the organization are another source. As the producers of the goods or services of the organization they certainly influence what is actually accomplished. In this sense, the members have a voice in goal definition. A third source might be the persons for whom the goods or services are produced, the people who buy the food, the symphony listeners, and the bus riders. By their demands these persons exert an influence on organizational goals. Finally, society exerts pressure on the goals of the organization. It can influence an auto company to include the production of safe, smog-free cars in its goal definition. It can exert strong influences on the choice of goals of educational institutions.

In one sense, however, who defines the goal is an unimportant question. If we wish to assess the effectiveness of an organization, we can do so only after we understand the organizational goal. It is important to note that various persons will probably disagree about the goals and to realize that many of the answers to our questions about organizations will vary according to our specification of the goal. In fact, when considering the problems raised here and in his organizational experiences, the reader should remember that many disagreements related to organizational issues could be easily resolved if there were agreement on the goals. For example, the Product A supervisor in ORG informs the personnel staff that vacancies in his department should be filled by individuals who can produce the greatest amount of units in the shortest amount of time. Product B supervisor informs personnel that vacancies should be filled only by those people who can produce high quality goods. There is a conflict between the supervisors with respect to the type of individual wanted, although both types of individuals hired may yield equal amounts of profits. If there were agreement on the level of quality desired, there could be agreement on the type of worker hired.

Organizational Effectiveness

Once organizational goals are specified, it is necessary to determine whether the organization effectively fulfills its goals. How well has the organization achieved its goals? Is the organization viable? These questions pertain to the organization as a unit and will be considered here. Individual effectiveness, which as we have already indicated can conflict with organizational effectiveness, will be discussed in Chapter Four.

Many dimensions or criteria of organizational effectiveness have been identified (Campbell, 1973; Mahoney & Weitzel, 1969; Seashore & Yuchtman, 1967). Table 2.1 contains a partial list of dimensions of organizational effectiveness adapted from Campbell (1973). These criteria can serve as units in theoretical statements pertaining to organizational effectiveness.

TABLE 2.1. *Organizational effectiveness measures.*

Overall effectiveness. The degree to which the organization is accomplishing all its major tasks or achieving all its objectives. A general evaluation that takes in as many single criteria as possible and results in a general judgment about the effectiveness of the organization.

Quality. The quality of the primary service or product provided by the organization. This may take many operational forms, primarily determined by the *kind* of product or service provided by the organization.

Productivity. The quantity of or volume of the major product or service that the organization provides.

Readiness. An overall judgment concerning the probability that the organization could successfully perform some specified task if asked to do so.

Efficiency. A ratio that reflects a comparison of some aspect of unit performance to the costs incurred for that performance. Examples: dollars per single unit of production, amount of down time, and degree to which schedules, standards of performance, or other milestones are met.

Profit or return. The return on the investment used in running the organization from the owners' point of view. The amount of resources left after all costs and obligations are met, sometimes expressed as a percentage.

Growth. An increase in such things as manpower, plant facilities, assets, sales, profits, market share, and innovations. A comparison of an organization's present state with its own past state.

Turnover or retention. Frequency or amount of voluntary terminations.

Absenteeism. The frequency of occasions of personnel being absent from the job.

Accidents. Frequency of on-the-job accidents resulting in down time or recovery time.

Morale. Morale is a group phenomenon involving extra effort, goal communality, and feelings of belonging. Groups have some degree of morale, while individuals have some degree of satisfaction.

Evaluations by external entities. Evaluations of the organization or organizational unit by those individuals and organizations with which it interacts. Loyalty to, confidence in, and support given the organization by such groups as suppliers, customers, stockholders, enforcement agencies, and the general public.

In this chapter we deal with the problems involved in constructing an organization. These problems are seldom faced in that context, since each organization is constructed only once. But they recur, since all organizations are constantly in the process of reconstruction and growth. If there is any characteristic that is true of all organizations, it is that they undergo change. Though change may occur more slowly in some organizations than others, no organization can remain constant. It must adapt to shifts in power, purpose, and structure to reflect changes within the societal environment within which it exists. Organizational evolution and growth require us to address some of the problems basic to the construction of an organization. How large should the organization be? What should the structure of the organization be in terms of communication flow, authority, and responsibility? By what processes should decisions be made? How should the work be organized? In this section we suggest some of the theoretical units and empirical indicators which must be considered if such questions are to be studied scientifically.

There are many characteristics or dimensions which could be considered when describing organizations. In this chapter we will discuss those which should be considered when an organization as a whole is being studied. These organizational characteristics are often used as theoretical units in studies relating one to another or to other types of theoretical units (for example, attitudes and performance). Theoretical statements could be formulated to relate organizational size and leadership style, organizational shape and worker attitudes, degree of organizational centralization and performance, and so on.

Physical Dimensions—Within-Organization Comparisons

Within an organization there are several physical characteristics which might serve as theoretical units and have significant impact on the functioning of all or part of the organization. An obvious within-organization variable is *hierarchical levels.* From our chart of the Old Reliable Gadget company (see p. 16) we can see how members of the organization are stratified. By convention, the executive level, or the level with the ultimate authority, is placed at the top of such a chart and is called the top of the organization. The stratum which is furthest removed from the executive level is considered the bottom. Hierarchical level comparisons between blue-collar versus white-collar workers and upper management versus middle versus lower management have been made with respect to job attitudes and reward preferences. There are important differences between various organizational levels which will influence characteristics of the tasks at each level and how these tasks are performed. If we are concerned about the way that information is transmitted within the organization we may want to measure the number of upward and downward interpersonal contacts at each level. Or we may want to investigate differences in the content of upward and downward contacts at each level. In any event, there may be times when it will be helpful to consider levels as an important within-organization variable.

Another important intraorganizational unit is whether an organizational role is a *staff* position or part of the *line* or chain of command of the regular hierarchy. Members of the regular chain of command, who are directly concerned with production, are organizational *line members* (for example, the production manager, product supervisor, and foremen of ORG). Members who function throughout the organization as specialists or aides providing auxiliary services to the line members are called *staff members* (for example, E.D.P. consultant or assistant to the president of ORG). The occupants of line and staff roles may have very different relationships to the other members of the organization and to each other. In fact, Position A may be in a staff (advisory) relationship to Position B with respect to activity X, but Position B is in a staff relationship to Position A with respect to activity Y. Classification into line or staff can act as one theoretical unit and be related to other theoretical units such as attitudes, tenure, and number of within-organization communications.

A third variable which may affect the way that persons function in certain organizational situations is the *span of control*, the number of persons supervised by a single supervisor. Each shop foreman in ORG may supervise 7 or 8 workers, whereas the sales managers supervise from 14 to 19 salesmen. Though it is certain that the span of control can be an important influence, there is no way to generalize about the optimum number of persons to supervise. That number depends on the technology of the work being done, the characteristics of the workers being supervised, the extent to which the supervisor is required to participate in nonsupervisory tasks, and the management philosophy, among other factors. The number of persons optimally supervised, therefore, must be established for each particular situation.

A fourth intraorganizational characteristic, *subunit function*, can also be treated as a theoretical unit. The fact that many organizations form themselves into subgroups with differentiated tasks is often of real importance. Lawrence and Lorsch (1967) have pointed out the many concomitant differences of such division. Subunits which might have started with different parts of the same task are quite likely, over time, to develop goals which conflict with those held by the other subunits. Subunits charged with production responsibilities, for example, are concerned with the here-and-now filling of current product orders, whereas the research and development subunit is trying to produce products which will have a market potential in two (or five) years (with little thought to the technological changes required). It is little wonder that these subunits cannot agree on the priorities for use of company resources. The more control each subunit has over its own operation, the less likely that its goals will coincide with the original, overall purpose. The production subunit will be oriented primarily toward the demands which it receives from within the company, marketing will be focused on the demands of the customers, and research and development will be sensitive to related scientific fields. And of course, subunits with different functions will also differ in such characteristics as size, member characteristics (education, age, experience), and organizational structure.

The final intraorganizational characteristic or theoretical unit which we will consider is actually a set of variables, *environmental conditions*. Many physical environmental characteristics have been researched to determine if they have an effect on the dependent variables of job performance and satisfaction. Perhaps the popularity of this research can be explained in part by the fact that it is relatively easy to make changes in the work environment, and if such changes bring about improved performance, they can be easily instituted.

An early set of studies, initially concerned with environmental factors, was conducted at the Hawthorne plant of the Western Electric Company (Roethlisberger & Dickson, 1939). The Hawthorne Studies investigated the relationships between various characteristics of the work situation and productivity. The first of these studies was meant to demonstrate little more than the relationship between level of illumination and productivity. However, as the lighting was manipulated to vary the amount of illumination, no simple relationship emerged. In some cases, production increases were as great for groups which experienced no change in lighting as they were for groups with increased illumination. In other cases, persons who had increased productivity after illumination had been increased in their work area remained at the higher productivity level even after the lighting was returned to a lower level.

This study is a good example of the possibility for confounding results. One reason that the hypothesized relationship between illumination and productivity was unsupported was that social and attitude factors had not been considered (controlled). Productivity was influenced by the introduction of researchers and the increased monitoring of performance more than by the changes in illumination. That is, the workers in the plant perceived the research as management concern for their welfare and consequently increased production. The phenomenon of change in a dependent variable induced by the mere fact that research is being conducted has come to be called the Hawthorne Effect. In general, none of the Hawthorne Studies showed that environmental factors had any strong influence on work performance. However, these studies are historically significant in the field of industrial psychology. Changes in the dependent variable can occur for reasons other than those which the researcher thinks are operating. (This again points out the difficulty researchers have in identifying all of the relevant variables.) Consequently, the chances of generalization of research results from one situation to another are limited. A corollary is that social and psychological characteristics can overwhelm the effect of environmental variations.

One method for eliminating the Hawthorne Effect is to use unobtrusive measures. As presented by Webb, Campbell, Schwartz, and Sechrest (1966), unobtrusive measures are those which do not affect, by the act of assessment, the value of the unit being measured. In the social sciences, *obtrusive* measures (which do affect the thing being measured) are abundant. By questioning a worker about his attitudes toward his job, we may change those attitudes. If we institute visible measurements of individual worker output, we may change individual productivity. Whenever possible, therefore, we should use unobtrusive measures for research purposes.

For nonresearch purposes, it may be appropriate to use obtrusive measures of performance. Obtrusive display of the amount of goods sold might encourage salesman performance. Obtrusive camera surveillance of employees in a warehouse may discourage employee theft. Though the obtrusive measurements seem to achieve the objectives, we can never be fully confident that the changes are truly a function of our measures because no research design was used. It is possible that the performance changes are naturally occurring events and would have taken place had we not displayed the sales records or introduced the cameras. A more confident interpretation could be made had we used control groups.

Investigations of the effects of environmental characteristics over wide ranges of both physical and mental work tasks have left many unresearched questions and few generalizable results. It does seem, however, that significant effects on satisfaction and performance are caused only by extreme environmental conditions—light too weak to illuminate work materials, noise so loud that prolonged exposure causes ear damage, temperature low enough to lessen coordination, and so on. This is not to say that environmental factors cannot influence performance and attitudes on some specific task, but knowledge about such influence is best learned from research on that specific situation. Some of the environmental variables which have been researched include noise and vibration, temperature, humidity, air pressure, colors, music, and illumination.

Recent research suggests that the social environment may be an important influence. Investigation of the effects of the physical arrangement of space and interpersonal interaction among workers has just begun (Hall, 1966; Sommer, 1969), and there are indications that various territorial and interpersonal arrangements may be quite important. The physical distance between workers and their spatial relationships (face to face, side by side, and so on) can influence patterns of interpersonal interaction.

Physical Dimensions—Between-Organization Comparisons

There are also physical differences between organizations which have an impact on their method and effectiveness of performance. These characteristics can also serve as theoretical units when comparing one organization to another. One such unit is *size*. The appropriate gauge of size depends on the comparisons which are of greatest interest. Usually the number of members is used as an empirical indicator of the size of an organization, but it is sometimes useful to consider the amount of economic worth, the number of customers, or the amount of space controlled. Our choice of empirical indicator will influence the empirical results of research in which size is a theoretical unit.

Though most organizations try to expand, there are some negative correlates of increased size. The disadvantages include greater efforts to coordinate activities of subunits of the organization, less recognition by the individual member of his contribution to the organization, greater impersonality on the part of "specialists" who make decisions about unknown persons far removed from them in the organization, and the tendency toward inflexible regulations.

Another physical dimension which can be compared between organizations is *shape*. In this context, shape refers to the hierarchical structure of the organization. This is usually described by a dimension which runs from tall to flat. A tall organization is one which has many hierarchical levels; a flat organization has few. However, this judgment is dependent on the size of the organization. An organization with 20 members and five hierarchical levels would be considered tall, but a 10,000-member organization with five levels would be considered flat. The shape of the organization is related to the amount of autonomy and control a member feels. With a tall organization a member may feel that he is far removed from contact with decision-making officers (and vice versa). In a flat organization a member may feel frustration because of lack of contact with all or key members on the same level.

A concept related to organizational shape is the relative degree of *centralization*. Centralization is defined by some researchers as the extent to which decision making is restricted to a localized set of people; others have defined it as the geographical dispersion of organizational subunits. Though not identical, these definitions are often related. As an example of a relatively centralized corporation, we could consider one with headquarters in Chicago where a few people make policies and procedures for all subunits throughout the country. In contrast, a relatively decentralized organization would be one in which decisions are made in various regions of the country by various people for their respective subunits.

Psychological Dimensions

There are some dimensions which pertain to organizations but are more characteristic of its members than they are of the organization itself. These characteristics can have an effect on the worker satisfaction and performance even though they are not physical or structural. They are a part of workers' perceptions of the organization, reactions to the organization, and affects toward the organization—all constitute the workers' psychological response to the organization.

The first is the degree of *conflict* between the goals of the individual and the organization. For example, one of an individual's work goals may be to establish friendships on the job. This conflicts with the organization's goal of maximum productivity because overzealous workers may be envied or disliked by their peers. To the extent that this individual feels that organizational goals can be achieved only at the expense of his personal goals, both satisfaction and performance could be expected to be low. To find out if this is, in fact, the case, some measurement would need to be made of the goal conflict. First we would need to assess whether the individual perceives that there is a conflict between his and the organization's goals. Second, we should assess the way the conflict is resolved by the individual—would he leave the organization, change his goals, change his perception of the organization's goals, or would he just decide to continue in a state of conflict?

A second important psychological characteristic of organizations is the manner in which *leadership* is exercised. Recent thought in this area suggests that the style of effective leadership will differ according to organizational context. The leadership style which would make a person an effective football coach may be different from the style necessary to direct a research laboratory. Both of these are likely to differ from the style which would be best for a hospital administrator.

To measure leadership behavior it is important to designate the perspective from which the behavior is being evaluated. Leader behavior can be described by *subordinates, peers, the leader himself, superiors,* or *expert observers.* It is important to realize that persons in each of these relationships to the leader may report different behaviors for the leader because each sees his behavior from a different viewpoint. Empirical indicators of leadership behavior could be *feelings* toward the leader's behavior, *responses* of other persons to the leader's behavior, or *descriptions* of the leader's activities—how do you feel when your leader corrects your work; what do you do when your leader corrects your work; how often does your leader correct your work?

Several studies have pointed out the usefulness of conceptualizing leader behavior in two categories—activities oriented to the task and activities oriented to the interpersonal relationships within the work group (Bass, 1960; Fiedler, 1967; Stogdill & Coons, 1957). An item format used to assess these activities asks subordinates to indicate the frequency with which their supervisors engage in specified behaviors (Stogdill & Coons, 1957). An item which has been used for task orientation is: He sees to it that people under him are working up to their limits. An item which has been used for interpersonal relations orientation is: He makes those under him feel at ease when talking with him. Task orientation implies a concern for achieving the work goals, whereas an interpersonal orientation implies a concern for the relationships among the members of the work group.

To measure the organizational context or the characteristics of the situation within which the leadership is occurring, Fiedler (1967) has suggested that we look at the interpersonal relationships among the group members, the amount of structure in the task, and the amount of power held by the leader. These three factors determine the favorableness of the situation for the leader. In situations of different favorableness, different leadership styles are relatively more effective. And there is no set of leader behaviors which will produce effective performance in all situations. To find out what behavior is most effective in a specific situation, it is necessary to investigate that situation.

The final psychological characteristic we will discuss is the psychological *climate*, or the character of the organization as it is perceived by the members and the general public. That is, it is the experienced or phenomenological organization. Just as we might describe the personality of a person, we can talk about the personality, or climate, of an organization. It is observed through the descriptive words of the members: "things are tense at the office"; "it's a very fair place to work"; or "that's a very progressive company." To be sure, all members of the organization will not agree in their descriptions of the climate. To some it will appear rigid and to others it will appear flexible; to some it will appear insensitive and to others responsive; to some it will appear destructive and to others constructive. To persons at different hierarchical levels, in different functional subunits, or with varying years of experience or association in the organization, the psychological climate may be quite disparate. How, then, do we obtain information about the general climate of an organization?

To begin with (and this point should be remembered throughout this book), whenever we group data to get general information, we give up specific information. When we place people in categories or groups and then use characteristics of the groups, we ignore information about the individual differences among group members. For example, if most workers (the mode) in ORG describe it as "efficient" and we use the term to describe the organization, we cannot assume that *all* of the workers agree. We should avoid the common error of automatically grouping data without first considering whether it is the general information which we want. However, there are many occasions for which a summary statement is appropriate. If we asked all of the members of ORG to describe what kind of a place it is to work, we might get several books full of descriptive data. We would probably not be able to use so much information unless we had some way to reduce it to the general, or typical, or average descriptions.

To facilitate the pooling of the information we obtain, it is helpful to collect the information in a standard way. If we ask one worker to tell us what his work place is like and we ask another to tell us what he likes best about his work place, we cannot compare their answers to see if they have a similar view. Their answers may differ simply because they are responding to different questions. Whether we have the organizational occupants fill out a log or diary form, respond to an interview, or answer a questionnaire, we must be sure that they are all responding to the same questions. Then we can pool the information which they provide to see the extent to which perceptions of the organization agree.

One method for obtaining organizational climate descriptions is to give members a long list of adjectives and then ask them to indicate the degree to which each adjective describes their organization (Graham, 1970). Such adjectives as "authoritarian," "crooked," "enterprising," "progressive," and "versatile" have been used. It might be useful for an individual who is considering joining to know that *most* of the members of the organization perceive it as a cold, rigid, nonsupportive place to work. Alternatively, such information might induce the policy makers of the organization to change the psychological climate.

A final consideration in this section on organizational dimensions is that there is constant interaction between individual characteristics, the characteristics of tasks being performed, the organizational characteristics, and the characteristics of the economic and social society in which the organization exists. Whenever there are changes in some of these characteristics, there are likely to be changes in others. If a production process for the workers in the Product A section of ORG is made more automated it may require less supervision. This in turn might influence section A workers' attitudes toward their immediate supervisors as well as their perceptions of the entire organization (climate). If the changes produced higher quality units with less worker effort, the result could be a change in the prestige of the section A workers as viewed by the general community and other workers in ORG. Finally, there may be changes in the attitudes of workers in *other* departments and in the tasks of some departments in relation to the services they provide for section A (for example, selection and training procedures).

Communications

We have indicated that organizations are complex systems of interactions. There are units within organizational structures which have units within themselves, and the result is a system of differentiated units. Each unit, however, specializes in its own activities and uses a communication system to coordinate its efforts. For example, the communications systems of the payroll and operations staffs in ORG may differ though they are both subunits of the larger unit, the accounting department.

Communications is an aspect of organizations which deserves special consideration since it embodies the process which allows the organization to operate. Without communication which allows the coordination of the activities of its members, there is no organization. Communications link individuals to individuals, groups of workers to other groups of workers with the same and different functions, and the organization to individuals and groups outside the organization. The type of communication system may serve as a theoretical unit in a theoretical statement. For example, we might state that different *communication systems* will lead to different *worker attitudes*, or that different *communication systems* will function more *efficiently* in organizations with different *structures*. We will examine two aspects of communications: the flow of communications and the effects of communications.

Measuring the Flow: Who, What, and How

In measuring the flow of communications, we are concerned with who initiates and who receives the communication, what type of information is communicated, and which network is used (and how) for communication. In other words, we are concerned with the *pattern* (who and how) and *content* (what) of communication processes. We can answer several questions by examining characteristics of communications flows.

All communications consist of an initiator (the "who") and at least one receiver (unless the message is lost or misplaced). Communications can be informal or formal. Those which convey official information or instructions are formal, whereas casual or unofficial communications are informal. Whether the communication is formal or informal may depend on whether it is a line to line, staff to staff, or line to staff interaction.

The "what" aspect of our problem can be approached by examining Guetzkow's (1965) qualitative classification of communication networks. These networks range from very formal and structured to very informal, depending on the purpose of the communication. Essentially, there are five qualitative networks:

1. *Authority networks.* Authority messages are concerned with directives and commands and are characterized by directionality. The message usually flows vertically within the organization via a prescribed route from the top of the authority structure to those below. This type of communication usually is direct, short, formal, and authenticated. An example of an authority message would be

a directive from the office of O. L. Reliable, President of ORG, requesting that all production units work overtime to meet production schedules. This message would go from O. L. Reliable to the vice-president to the production manager to the product supervisors to the staff foremen to the shop foremen and finally to the workers.

2. *Information exchange.* Information exchanges are concerned with knowledge about the state of affairs operating in the organization. These communications flow vertically, from top to bottom or bottom to top, or laterally. Information exchanges often will accompany authority messages and, just as often, lead to confusion as to whether they are authority or information messages. The group most often associated with information exchanges, however, is the staff members. For example, the finance manager of ORG may send a message to the E.D.P. consultant informing him that salaries will be paid monthly rather than bi-weekly and requesting him to make the necessary data-processing changes.

3. *Task-expertise.* This network is concerned with the communication of technical knowledge. Again, staff members are most often associated with this network. For example, one member of the research and development unit of ORG may inform another member that he has discovered a new chemical which could be used in the production process.

4. *Friendship.* These networks usually contain an affective component and serve as a means of interaction among small groups. An example would be a telephone call from the finance manager of ORG to the marketing manager offering a ride to the monthly managers' luncheon. Since there can be an affect in messages involving authority, information exchange, and task-expertise, the communication channels of friendship overlap with the channels of the previous networks.

5. *Status.* These informal networks serve to establish interrelationships among members of the organization. Examples of status networks are messages that relay knowledge about who goes to see whom, who has lunch in the Executive Club with whom, who used the company car, and so on. These examples can easily be gathered by unobtrusive measures.

Whether the communication process is simultaneous or serial provides a partial answer to the "how" of the problem. In essence, we are concerned with timing, or the sequence of the communication. That is, in serial communications, A tells B who in turn tells C. In simultaneous communications A tells B and C at approximately the same time and via the same mode of communication (oral or written). Timing is important for several reasons. First, it can influence the functioning of individuals in their relation to each other. Time lags can develop and problems of coordination can arise. However, appropriate timing is often restricted by physical distance; that is, it is often difficult to coordinate activities by simultaneous communication when the members are located in different parts of the organization. Consequently, what might be intended as a simultaneous communication may, in effect, be a serial flow. Second, serial communications often lead to omissions and distortions. Hence, in addition to physical distance, the number of participants in the communication will determine the appropriate form of timing.

Procedures for Measuring the Flow of Communications in Field Settings

The measurement of communications patterns and content is a difficult task and consequently often not very rigorous. The methods we have are imprecise, but they do provide general pictures of the communications flow.

Living-in. In this technique, the researcher becomes part of the organizational unit (for example, a worker in Product A supervisor's group) in which the communications analysis is being undertaken. The researcher thus has first-hand, though subjective, knowledge about the communications patterns. This procedure is costly and time consuming, and the researcher often is not accepted by the other members of the unit. As a result, he may receive a distorted picture of the communications process. Also, since the researcher is actively involved in the work of his position, his observations are limited to those units with which he can maintain physical contact. The result of this procedure is a limited and possibly biased picture of the content and pattern of communications.

Indirect analysis. This technique is used to make inferences about communications *between* units. For example, we may be interested in the pattern of communications between the Product A supervisor and the research and development staff of ORG. Indirect analysis is usually carried on by having the researcher observe the exchange between the units. Observation and self-reports reveal the amount of time and pattern of communications between units but do not necessarily reveal such information as the content. The use of observation and self-reports can lead to distorted and exaggerated pictures of the process.

Diary. One form of self-report requires that the participants keep a communications log. The record keeping, done on a standard form, can be full time or based on randomly selected time-periods of a worker's schedule. In addition, the entire work group or a randomly sampled group of participants are used. In either case, this technique provides partial information on the amount, pattern, and content of communications. This technique, like all self-report procedures, relies on the willingness and accuracy of the participants.

Duty study. One form of observation requires the researcher to record all communications which flow past one particular spot in the organization. For example, we can observe all communications to and from a sales manager's office. Information is obtained with respect to amount, content, and pattern for that location; but no information is obtained with respect to the *general* pattern of communication throughout the organization. In addition, the technique can be very costly and time consuming. The researcher should resort to random sampling of days and times for that particular point of interest. There is also the possibility that the researcher will be obtrusive and bias the content and pattern of communications.

Cross-section analysis. This procedure involves random sampling of time and day and can be extended to random sampling of locations. For example, observations may be made on the personnel staff on Monday morning, the advertising staff on Tuesday, the legal department on Thursday afternoon, and so on. An overall picture of the pattern of the communication system can be obtained but, again, the observer may be obtrusive.

Episodic communication channels in organizations—ECCO analysis. The focus in ECCO analysis (Davis, 1953) is on one particular bit of information as it passes through the entire organization. For example, we can observe a directive that originates in the president's office and filters down to the workers in each production unit. Each recipient indicates the source of the information that he has received and the pattern of communication is identified. An advantage is that experimental information can be inserted at any point, or one can observe a real bit of information as it flows routinely and regularly. But, of course, only one bit of information is observed (an authority message, for example) at one time.

Sociometric techniques. In this procedure, members of an organizational unit indicate sources for different information and problems with certain initiators and/or receivers. Although information about both pattern and content is obtained, the procedure often relies on the recall accuracy of the participants and is subject to omissions, distortions, and misperceptions.

Procedures for Measuring the Flow of Communications in Laboratories

There are several patterns, or *linkages*, which can be formulated and evaluated in the laboratory. By investigating linkage systems in the laboratory, we can more easily control *who* receives *what* by *how*. Attention is focused on the effects of the linkage systems or such dependent variables as attitudes or performance. Some linkage systems investigated by Leavitt (1951) and others are shown in Figure 2.1. The basic differentiating characteristic of the several linkage systems is centrality or peripherality. That is, in some linkage systems—the "Y" and wheel, for example—one person is central and everyone else is peripheral. The other linkage systems have all members in about the same degree of centrality. A bit of information is experimentally inserted at a particular point in the linkage and the attitudes (satisfaction) and performance (omissions, distortions, and so on) are assessed. Though the laboratory studies of linkage systems provide a great deal of control over the who, what, and how of communications, there are problems in generalizing from these studies to field situations. Systems of communications are rarely so neat in an on-going organization, and the laboratory tasks often have little significance for the participants.

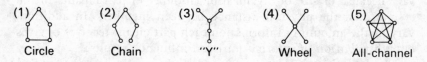

FIGURE 2.1. *Linkage systems.*

Measuring the Effects: Variables—Independent and Dependent

The independent variable is generally an aspect of the communications system (or linkage system, or network) that is initiated in the organization: (1) *frequency* of communication between or within units; (2) *content* (authority, information, task expertise, or friendship); (3) *technology* (oral or written, a dittoed or handwritten statement, one message placed in a strategic spot or sent to each individual); (4) *level* (within unit from top to bottom, between unit from top of unit to bottom of other unit or vice versa, line to staff or staff to line, and so on). An example of a theoretical statement using two of these characteristics as theoretical units is *"Frequency of communications between organizational units* is greater for *information messages* than *friendship messages."* The statement implies that there are more information than friendship exchanges between, for example, production unit A and production unit B.

The effects of the various communications networks are usually measured on two dependent variables, *attitude* and *performance.* A communications system can affect the group morale and attitudes toward the job, the leadership, and one's peers. Likewise, individual and group performance can be affected. Such variables as distortion of communications, omissions, and perception of the communication and/or communicator could be measured and related to the previously mentioned independent variables. A theoretical statement could say, for example, that there are more distortions in authority messages than in information messages.

There are other variables which researchers may wish to consider when studying communications. Whether the communication goes from top to bottom, bottom to top, or side to side (*direction of flow*) can be directly related to the previously mentioned independent and dependent variables. The degree to which members of the organization have access to each other for communication purposes (*openness of channels*) may also be an important variable. Results may vary because of size of organization, number of participants in the system, and the physical distance between members. In addition, varying the amount of information each participant receives or gives out (*distribution of information*) can influence results.

Each of the variables mentioned in this section can be studied in a simple relationship—that is, one variable in relation to another—or several may be looked at in combination. An example of the latter is the relationship between *amount of distortion* and *direction of flow* in organizations of different *size.*

Decision Processes

We have focused, in the preceding sections, on organizational structures, characteristics, and properties. A major determinant of the success of our organization is the decision-making processes. How decisions get made, of course, is influenced by organizational characteristics and communication processes. Just as properties of a communication system can serve as theoretical units, so can properties of a decision-making system.

Portions of Decision Process to Be Investigated

The first stage in decision making is the recognition that a problem exists or that action has to be taken. Subsequent steps are important to the decision-making sequence whether it involves everyday actions or specific problems. Specific problems must be recognized and defined before they can be solved: the budget, selection procedures, training programs, incentive policies, and job redesign, for example. These are nonroutine problems with major consequences.

Once the need to act or the problem is recognized, the decision maker must find solutions. It is at this point that we should distinguish between *individual decision making* and *organizational decision making*. The latter is concerned with the organizational structure and the formal decision-making model (a participative vs. a hierarchical decision-making model). Whether one or several persons make the decision depends on the organizational structure and the decision-making model employed. The model prescribes at what levels decisions are made, whether decisions are made at corporate headquarters (centralized) or regional offices (decentralized), and so on. Individual decision making, on the other hand, is concerned with the *strategy* an individual uses in attacking and solving his particular problem. Regardless of where in the organization the decision is being made, the individual decision strategy is determined by how an individual uses the information available to him. The organizational decision-making model and individual decision-making strategies are interdependent. For example, if many people participate in the decision-making process, more information is potentially available to a given individual than if he had to solve the problem by himself.

In finding solutions for our problem, there are two general strategies (Feldman & Kanter, 1965) that one can use, both dependent on how well the problem is defined. If the problem and goals to be achieved are well defined, one can *work backward*. The decision maker needs only consider those alternatives that lead to a desired terminal state. If the problem is to obtain workers with a specified set of work skills, we can consider three alternatives: hire people who already have the required skills; train people to meet the skill requirements; or use some combination of selection and training. If, on the other hand, a problem exists but the desired state is vague or even unknown, one can *work forward*. This procedure requires examination of many alternatives, each of which is explored in depth. If a decision must be made as to how to allot production resources among several products, careful examination must be made of the costs of resources and the market potential for many alternative product allotment combinations. (In this case, the desired state is maximum return to the organization, but that is unknown.)

It is possible to combine working forward with working backward. Regardless of the strategy, however, the result of stage two is a list of alternative solutions. Consequently, stage three focuses on selecting the best solution. One way to assess the best solution is to formulate all the alternatives and their respective consequences in a *payoff matrix* (see Figure 2.2). Each alternative can result in one or a series of terminal states, or results. The body of the matrix indicates the values (v) of a particular alternative-state condition. These values can be based on objective (monetary or production) or subjective (social value) considerations.

STATES (RESULTS)

1 2 3 4 . . .

ALTERNATIVES	
1	V_{11} V_{21} V_{31} V_{41} V . . .
2	V_{12} V_{22} V_{32} V_{42} V . . .
3	V_{13} V_{23} V_{33} V_{43} V . . .
4	V_{14} V_{24} V_{34} V_{44} V . . .
. . .	V . . .

FIGURE 2.2. *Payoff matrix.*

Suppose additional personnel are needed to fill openings in the computer operations staff of ORG. The personnel manager's problem is how to obtain these additional employees. Various selection strategies are listed in the "alternatives" column of Figure 2.3. Each alternative can be evaluated with respect to its effects on various outcomes for the organization (listed in the top row of Figure 2.3).

ALTERNATIVES	STATES (RESULTS)				
	TRAINING COSTS	SELECTION COSTS	EXPECTED TENURE	PUBLIC RELATIONS	FIRST YEAR PRODUCTIVITY
1. Hiring skilled people with experience	none	high	long term	minimum	maximum
2. Hiring un-skilled and giving training	medium to high	low	long term	moderate	minimum
3. Hiring skilled people without experience	low	medium	short term	minimum	moderate to maximum
4. Hiring disad-vantaged groups	low (federal aid)	low	?	maximum	minimum

FIGURE 2.3. *Payoff matrix: Hiring computer operators for ORG.*

The body of the matrix shows the subjective interpretation of the benefits and costs for each of the alternative selection strategies as given by the personnel manager. For example, hiring according to alternative 1 (skilled people with experience) would result in high costs for selection procedures because skilled and experienced people demand higher initial wages than others, and the competition for these people in the labor market is more intense. Hiring according to alternative 3 (skilled people without experience) may result in short-term employment because once experience is acquired by these people they are in greater demand from other companies. These people may be younger than the experienced persons and taking the job only to gain experience. Alternative 4 (disadvantaged groups) does not incur training costs, because federal aid can be obtained for the training of disadvantaged groups. However, it is difficult for this personnel manager to make a prediction about expected tenure. On the one hand he knows that there is a large turnover in many programs hiring disadvantaged persons. On the other hand, he knows that there is a tendency for persons to stay longer in the organizations that have trained them.

The other alternative-state combinations can be similarly interpreted as the personnel manager's subjective judgments, but objective values may be obtainable for some combinations. The choice of an alternative will depend not only on the personnel manager's assessment of values but also on his assessment of the relative importance of the various states. If he believes that public relations is very important to ORG, the attractiveness of alternative 4 will be increased. Finally, it is possible that analysis of the matrix would indicate that more than one alternative should be adopted. This procedure does not eliminate the necessity for the decision maker to exercise his own judgment, but it does allow him to assess the alternatives systematically.

Further considerations in determining the inputs to the payoff matrix involve *a priori* and *a posteriori* decision-making probabilities. The point is that in decision making, the individual (usually subjectively) considers the probability of an occurrence given his pursual of a particular alternative; probability usually is dependent on past experiences. In essence, there is some certainty, risk, and uncertainty involved in each decision.

The final stage in the decision sequence is obtaining support for enactment of the decision. The likelihood of obtaining support can be contingent on the organizational decision-making model or structure (hierarchical or participative), and both the actual participants (the rank-and-file) and management personnel must support the decision to maximize chances for success.

Approaches for Analyzing Decision-Making Processes

We have examined several basic components of and approaches to individual decision making. The next concern is an examination of the formal decision-making process. We are interested in assessing (1) which process the decision maker employs (for example, working forward or working backward); (2) what information or variables are considered; (3) who, if anyone, is consulted by the decision maker; and (4) variables influencing the decision-making process (interval of time between recognizing problem and selecting a solution, interval of time between postulating an alternative for solving the problem and initiating action, personality characteristics of decision makers, and so on). To answer some of these questions, we can resort to several somewhat informal or subjective processes which usually are not rigorous in methodology. The variables mentioned in point 4 might act as theoretical units in theoretical statements about decision processes.

One way to examine the decision-making process is to use the techniques we mentioned when discussing communications procedures. Now, however, rather than focusing on the pattern and information content of a communication we are interested in the content and pattern of decisions. The communication techniques enable us to determine who is consulted in decision making, how information is gathered, and how actions are distributed.

A second approach is to interview the formal decision makers. But the interview as an information-gathering technique in decision-making processes has several problems. First, the interview can result in a biased interpretation or analysis—decision makers may distort and omit characteristics involved in their process. Sometimes persons are unable to explain what influenced them to choose a particular alternative. This problem arises in many situations where persons are required to explain or describe their behavior *after* they have acted. Second, it is difficult to interview everyone directly or indirectly involved. Considerations of time and effort may require the researcher to sample participants. And in some situations it may not be possible to determine all of the persons who have had an impact on a decision.

A third, more formal and objective approach is policy capturing (see Christal, 1968a, 1968b), which enables us to examine how individuals make a decision. For example, each of the five members of the personnel staff of ORG will independently examine the same information in the applications of 50 people for eight vacancies in the eastern salesman office. Using the policy-capturing method we obtain for *each* member of the personnel staff a statistical equation which indicates how he weighted and combined information to decide who should be hired. The equations are compared to assess how many hiring policies are operating. That is, we will determine if each staff member is considering the same information and placing similar importance on the various kinds of information. Do the staff value test scores, previous work experience, or personal information equally? Or do some staff base their decisions mostly on test scores whereas other staff base their decisions primarily on previous work experience and personal information? If each member is using a similar equation, one policy equation for the entire group is generated and used in the future. The ultimate benefit is that in new but similar situations the staff members do not have to review all information, but instead use an equation which incorporates the decision policy. Adoption of this equation avoids the problem of inconsistent members' use and evaluation of information.

The limits of policy capturing are obvious. First, if more than one policy equation is operating, discussion and compromise among the staff members is necessary. Second, policy capturing is best used for routine or simple situations where the information is fairly straightforward (as in the above example); equations are easily formed from these data. In contrast, a decision about expenditure of funds for various activities may be too complicated for a policy-capturing model. There are too many important variables and each would be difficult to quantify. Where policy capturing is appropriate, however, it provides information on the type and significance of the variables contributing to our decision.

A fourth approach to assessing the decision-making operation is simulation. In this procedure, we observe how an individual resolves a problem in a simulated situation. Such simulations are usually referred to as business games and are commonly used as training devices for managers. Business games simulate a total business environment, and the game play is divided into several operating or decision periods during which the individual(s) must make a wide range of decisions. Information about an individual's decision-making behavior can be obtained by observing him in the simulated environment. The utility of business games is limited by the fact that the decisions usually are in such functional areas as finance, marketing, production, and research and development. Also, the degree of simulation can influence the generalization of decision behavior to realistic situations.

Another simulation device is the "in-basket" test (Frederiksen, Saunders, & Ward, 1957), which is often used as a selection device for executive or leadership positions. The fundamental properties and characteristics of the in-basket test also can be used to examine the decision-making process. The in-basket test is basically situational and simulates important aspects of an administrator's job. The individual is given an "in-basket" with memos, letters, directives, and so on to which he must respond in a limited time period. He is evaluated on style (how) and content (what) of his responses. For decision-making purposes, one can examine the way information is utilized and the priorities set by the individual. Again, however, the fact that the individual is in a simulated or, in this case, test environment, may limit the generalization of decision-making behavior.

Characteristics of Decision Makers

We have examined the components of a decision process and how to investigate the way an individual makes a decision. There is, also, some research which characterizes decision makers based on theoretical postulates. We will briefly review the theories, not because of their value *per se* but because they indicate individual characteristics which influence the decision-making process.

Boulding (1958) has characterized one type of decision maker as "heroic man." This individual believes in pursuing strategies regardless of cost. Shubik (1958) cites "economic man," a rational person who constructs payoff matrices and chooses the strategy that promises the most valuable result. "Satisficing man" (Simon, 1957) is concerned with feasible, practical strategies which meet certain minimum criteria. The chosen strategy is "at least satisfactory" but is not necessarily the optimal strategy.

Given these hypothetical decision makers, several theoretical units can be investigated. In addition to ability characteristics, we can examine motivational variables, need for achievement and success, and such work values as need for status, prestige, security, and self-actualization. Also, risk-taking behavior and the need for conformity might be related to individual differences in decision making.

Organizational Decision-Making Models

In the preceding sections we have focused on individual decision making—that is, we have been concerned with one decision maker and his decision-making process. We have been concerned also with ways to examine his decision-making process and have noted some of the variables affecting individual decision making. The latter concerns are influenced by the organizational decision-making model, in particular, hierarchical (HIER) or participative decision making (PDM).

A hierarchical model exists when the decision maker and the action that carries out the decision are formally separate in the organizational structure. Simply, certain people make the decisions and certain other people act on or carry out the decision. For example, the shop foremen in ORG may establish work quotas for the workers. In a HIER decision-making model the workers are not consulted about the work quotas.

A participative decision-making model exists when there is formal involvement in the decision-making process by *all* individuals who will carry out the decision. The making and the carrying out of the decision involve the same people. Shop foremen and workers would jointly discuss and determine work quotas.

It should be noted that PDM and HIER are not mutually exclusive. Hierarchies exist in all organizations, but some allow for PDM at various levels in the hierarchy. Probably no organization operates entirely and consistently with one or the other of these models. Certain types of decisions should be made in a HIER model and others should be made with PDM. Arbitrary administrative details which have little impact on the workers' lives and decisions which must be made quickly might be decided in a HIER fashion. On the other hand, decisions which have an important effect on the workers might be made by PDM.

One advantage of PDM is that it allows for relatively more ego and need fulfillment. Low-level members might be less frustrated if they are allowed to participate in decision making. A second advantage is that PDM allows fuller utilization of manpower resources. With more people participating, more ideas and potential solutions

may be generated. A third advantage is greater cooperation and identification with the organization.

There are also advantages to the HIER decision-making model.
First, decisions can usually be made more quickly. Second, it is clear
who is responsible for the decisions that are made because responsibility and authority usually coincide. People are less likely to have
responsibility for decision areas in which others have the decision-
making authority. Third, the HIER model may produce less overt
conflict. Disagreements can arise during PDM discussions and the
decision may not be unanimously accepted, whereas in HIER, since
there is no participation in decision making, the possibility for overt
conflict is reduced.

The success of PDM or HIER is influenced by several variables,
many of which Lowin (1968) has delineated. Attitudinal variables
contribute a great deal to the success or failure of PDM or HIER.
For example, the accessibility of staff advice or the availability of
formal recognitions and financial remuneration affect PDM. These
factors must be consistent with each other if PDM is to be effective.
Those people participating (particularly at lower levels) should be
formally recognized for their contribution to decision making and
their salaries possibly could reflect this responsibility. In addition,
members should cooperate; whenever any of the participants in PDM
do not accept the results, there is a movement to HIER.

Motivational and personality variables also affect the success
of PDM and HIER. The motives of the participants will increase
or decrease the success of PDM, especially the relationship between
the individuals' and the organization's goals. The need for achievement, autonomy, power, self-actualization, and authoritarianism also
mediate the effectiveness of PDM and HIER.

Finally, there are social and technical or administrative variables
which can mediate effectiveness. For example, social pressures directly relate to PDM performance. With respect to technical administrative factors, number of levels in the organization influences PDM.
The more levels and issues, the greater the likelihood of its success.
These and the above-mentioned variables can serve as theoretical
units in theoretical statements pertaining to organizational decision-
making models. For example, "*Acceptance of a decision* in PDM
is related to *motivation level* of the participants," or "*Amount of
overt conflict* is related to the *decision-making model* (PDM or
HIER)."

Summary

In this chapter we have attempted to develop an organizational framework and to identify the important factors involved in organizational analysis. Many of these same factors must be considered as the on-going organization changes through time. The important considerations in organizational analysis are the *dimensions* of the organization: those characteristics that define the structure of the organization. And we must also consider the functioning processes involved in an organization—for example, the communications system and the decision-making model. Finally, to evaluate many of the theoretical statements that can be constructed in organizational analysis we have to consider the measures available to us or the ways of establishing empirical indicators (diaries, interviews, questionnaires, and so on) for the theoretical units. The concepts, issues, analyses, and procedures which will be discussed in the remaining chapters of this book occur in an organizational context, and the variables of this chapter must be kept in mind throughout. Again, the reader is reminded that organizations are complex interactions and the units, functions, and systems are interdependent.

References

Organizational Analysis

Bass, B. M. *Leadership, psychology, and organizational behavior.* New York: Harper, 1960.

Campbell, J. P. Research into the nature of organizational effectiveness: An endangered species? Paper presented at the Conference on Occupational Research and the Navy—Prospectus 1980, San Diego, 1973.

Fiedler, F. E. *A theory of leadership effectiveness.* New York: McGraw-Hill, 1967.

Forehand, G. A., & Gilmer, B. V. H. Environmental variation in studies of organizational behavior. *Psychological Bulletin,* 1964, **62,** 361–382.

Graham, W. K. A method for measuring the images of organizations. Paper presented at the meeting of the Western Psychological Association, Los Angeles, 1970.

Hall, E. T. *The hidden dimension.* Garden City, New York: Doubleday, 1966.

Korman, A. K. "Consideration," "initiating structure," and organizational criteria—a review. *Personnel Psychology,* 1966, **19,** 349–361.

Lawrence, P. R., & Lorsch, J. W. *Organization and environment: Managing differentiation and integration.* Boston: Harvard Graduate School of Business Administration, 1967.

Mahoney, T. A., & Weitzel, W. F. Managerial model of organizational effectiveness. *Administrative Science Quarterly,* 1969, **14,** 357–365.

Perrow, C. *Organizational analysis: A sociological view.* Belmont, Calif.: Wadsworth, 1970.

Porter, L. W., & Lawler, E. E., III. Properties of organization structure in relation to job attitudes and job behavior. *Psychological Bulletin,* 1965, **64,** 23–51.

Porter, L. W., & Steers, R. M. Organizational, work, and personal factors in employee turnover and absenteeism. *Psychological Bulletin,* 1973, **80,** 151–176.

Price, J. L. *The handbook of organizational measurement.* Lexington, Mass.: D. C. Heath, 1972.

Roethlisberger, F. J., & Dickson, W. J. *Management and the worker.* Cambridge, Mass.: Harvard University Press, 1939.

Seashore, S. E., & Yuchtman, E. Factorial analysis of organizational performance. *Administrative Science Quarterly,* 1967, **12,** 377–395.

Sommer, R. *Personal space; the behavioral basis of design.* Englewood Cliffs, N. J.: Prentice-Hall, 1969.

Stogdill, R. M., & Coons, A. E. *Leadership behavior: Its description and measurement.* Bureau of Business Research, Ohio State University, Columbus, Ohio, 1957, No. 88.

Townsend, R. *Up the organization.* Greenwich, Conn.: Fawcett, 1970.

Communications

Davis, K. A. A method of studying communication patterns in organizations. *Personnel Psychology,* 1953, **6,** 301–312.

Guetzkow, H. Communications in organizations. In J. G. March (Ed.), *Handbook of organizations.* Chicago, Ill.: Rand McNally, 1965. Pp. 534–573.

Leavitt, H. J. Some effects of certain communication patterns on group performance. *Journal of Abnormal and Social Psychology,* 1951, **46,** 38–50.

Decision Making

Boulding, K. E. *Skills of the economist.* Cleveland, Ohio: Howard Allen, 1958.

Christal, R. E. JAN: A technique for analyzing group judgment. *Journal of Experimental Education,* 1968, **36,** 24–27. (a)

Christal, R. E. Selecting a harem—and other applications of the policy-capturing model. *Journal of Experimental Education,* 1968, **36,** 35–41. (b)

Feldman, J., & Kanter, H. E. Organizational decision making. In J. G. March (Ed.), *Handbook of organizations.* Chicago, Ill.: Rand McNally, 1965. Pp. 614–649.

Frederiksen, N., Saunders, D. R., & Ward, B. The in-basket test. *Psychological Monographs,* 1957, **71,** No. 9 (Whole No. 438).

Lowin, A. Participative decision making: A model, literature critique, and prescriptions for research. *Organizational Behavior and Human Performance,* 1968, **3,** 68–106.

Miles, R. E. Human relations or human resources? *Harvard Business Review,* 1965, **43,** 148–163.

Shubik, M. Studies and theories of decision-making. *Administrative Science Quarterly,* 1958, **3,** 289–306.

Simon, H. A. Theories of decision-making in economics and behavioral science. *American Economic Review,* 1959, **49,** 253–283.

Simon, H. A. *Models of man: Social and rational.* New York: Wiley, 1957.

Tannenbaum, A. S. *Social psychology and the work organization.* Belmont, Calif.: Wadsworth, 1966.

chapter
three

Job Design and
Job Analysis

Too often, the jobs in an organization (the individual parts of the overall organizational goal) are regarded as absolute components which we must accept. Hence, we try to understand and describe the jobs (see the section on Job Analysis below), or we try to find or train people for them (see Chapters Five and Six). Though these activities are appropriate in certain circumstances, it is important to remember that the jobs themselves can be redefined. That is, the definition or specification of job activities can be changed. It is not only the new or the expanding company that is in a position to consider job definitions. Changes in technology, in the characteristics of the available work force, and in the policies of the organization also may make job redefinition appropriate.

Considerations in Job Design Decisions

Technological

Historically, job definition has centered around technological considerations—the ways tasks are performed. For example, the job definition must prescribe a technology which is economically feasible. That is, the completion of the task must not require more human effort than the general society believes the result to be worth. We could devise a technology which would satisfactorily complete the task of floor scrubbing but which would require so much human effort that we would not think it reasonable. Would you trade the equivalent of four days of human labor in order to have your floor cleaned with toothbrushes and art gum erasers? Such decisions are relative, of course; some women will pay twice as much for a hand-made original dress as they will for a machine-made copy.

Also, the job definition must prescribe a technology which is competitively feasible. If others can perform the same task with less effort and fewer resources, it may be impossible to find anyone willing to pay the higher price which you must charge. Thus, in very competitive industries a technological improvement by one producer is likely to be mirrored by similar job redefinitions among the competitors. Though any of the major car companies could probably produce autos of the same quality and in the same number without an assembly-line technology, the additional human effort required by another production method would doubtless necessitate such uncompetitive prices that the company would soon be out of business.

TIME AND MOTION STUDIES

One of the first systematic attempts to consider the methods of task performance was the time and motion study of manual tasks. Such studies were carried on as early as the beginning of the twentieth century by such researchers as Frederick Taylor (1947) and Frank and Lillian Gilbreth (1917). The objective of time and motion studies was to improve work methods by eliminating waste and inefficiency, by reducing costs, and by minimizing fatigue. Likewise, time and motion studies could be used to determine which of several alternative work methods for a given function will result in the least waste, inefficiency, cost, and fatigue. The results of the studies also served as a basis for training and were used in comparing different jobs.

The studies were undertaken to develop a set of standard motions for the accomplishment of a task and, subsequently, time standards for the performance of each motion. The original development of time and motion study techniques was based on the notion that labor costs per unit could be lowered *and* wages could be raised by finding ways for workers to produce more in less time. Unfortunately, the studies have been used sufficiently often as a means (or excuse) for work speedups and worker layoffs so that workers have become (justifiably) skeptical of the benefits which they might derive from them.

The procedures of a time and motion study are relatively straightforward. First, the researcher must choose the persons (the subjects in the investigation) to set the standard times and motion.

These people must be chosen so that they will provide information about *typical* performance, not about maximum performance. Work performance should be recorded at different segments of the day and week and over some extended periods of time.

The motions of the task must be analyzed in careful detail. This, of course, implies that the motions can be specified. Consideration of such factors as lifting, grasping, assembling, manipulating, positioning, and so on are involved in an assessment of task motions. Implicit in this assessment is an assumption of "one best way" of task performance. Time and motion studies have the explicit intention of establishing a standard set of procedures, not a variety of alternative methods. The task is analyzed into its component motions by trained observers, often with the help of slow-motion films which allow the analyst to watch repetitions of the performance in greater detail. After the individual motions have been identified, unnecessary motions may be removed, motions may be combined, and the sequence of motions may be altered; or alternative motions may be considered, but with the idea that the best one will be adopted and the others will be dropped.

After a set of motions has been selected, the time required for each is measured. Extremely sophisticated methods, including films and precision timing devices, are available for this step. The representative sample of workers performs each of the motions separately and the time necessary for each is determined. If any new motions have been incorporated, the timing should not be done until they have been learned. A time near or slower than average should probably be considered standard since any faster performance requirement would lead to an expectation that most workers would do poorer than the standard. When the time required for each step in the task has been established, simple addition provides the required time for the complete task.

If the reader has been following the presentation of these procedures with growing skepticism, it is probably justified. In the actual use of a time and motion study, some important allowances must be made. First, there are few tasks for which a single set of motions can be described as "the best." Different people effectively accomplish the simplest tasks in different ways. The Fosbury Flop of the 1968 Olympics demonstrated that an unorthodox method for jumping over a stick was very effective for Fosbury. In addition to making allowances for individual differences, alternative methods for accomplishing a task may be more productive and satisfying than repeating the same motions for an entire eight-hour work day.

Allowances should also be made in time standards. Analysis of the sample of workers used in research not only provides an average amount of time necessary for the task but also indicates the variations to be expected in the time required for performing a task. Depending on the skills, enthusiasm, and social pressure for (or against) production, there will be differences in the time taken by different workers. Personal needs and health may also affect a worker's performance during a particular time period.

Standards for production methods and time can be established, and the methods for studying these facets of performance may lead to improved task design. Time and motion studies, however, are better used to establish minimum and maximum standards than to set inflexible patterns. The studies provide a way for establishing how a task could be done. Study results will have an impact on such facets of work in an organization as how performance will be evaluated, what job applicants will be selected, what training will be given to the workers, how workers will be rewarded, and how meaningful the work will seem to the worker.

MAN-MACHINE SYSTEMS

A recent and primarily technologically oriented development is man-machine systems. A man-machine system can be defined as a combination of human(s) and equipment (mechanical, electronic, and so on) for the accomplishment of a task. A rider and his bicycle; the rowers, coxswain, and shell of a rowing team; and the production crew (cameramen, engineers, mike-boom operators) and transmitting equipment of a television station are man-machine systems.

The first step in establishing an effective man-machine system is to define the task. What is the expected output of the proposed system? The expected output is prescribed by the organization's goals and by its resources. Having established what must be done in the task as a whole, subparts of the task must be apportioned between men and machines in such a way as to take advantage of the special abilities of each. Men should be given those tasks which require evaluating nonstandard stimuli (handwritten messages), responding to unexpected contingencies (broken pipes), and making patterns from separate pieces of information (meteorological data). Machines, on the other hand, are often better at handling tasks which require strength (cutting granite); performing repeated, standardized motions (corking wine bottles); storing and retrieving large amounts of information (typesetting stock market reports); and making rapid calculations (computing).

There are two considerations when defining the human tasks of man-machine systems—physical requirements and psychological requirements. The physical requirements are the inputs, which the worker must sense, and the tasks, which the worker must perform. The nature of the input to the worker is an important problem which has received considerable research for specific tasks. The most usual inputs are visual and auditory—a worker reads a gauge or hears a warning buzzer. Studies can ascertain what gauge formations are most quickly and accurately read and have shown some common gauge designs are more time-consuming and error prone than alternatives. Auditory and tactile inputs also must be examined to determine if they effectively convey the necessary information to the worker.

The worker should be able to perform the required task with a minimum of error. Some system designs nearly force workers into errors. In the building in which the authors' offices are located, there is an elevator with the "Alarm" button adjacent to the "Open Door" button. Since the "Open Door" button is usually jabbed in a hurry as an occupant spies someone running to catch the elevator, "alarms" ring frequently. Equipment controls which the worker must use in his task performance should not only be designed to avoid such errors but to provide ease of operation. Controls for many machines utilize color and shape codes to facilitate recognition and operation.

The psychological requirements of tasks, which involve both personal and social factors, also must be considered when designing man-machine systems. The job should be appropriate to the skills and desires of the worker, within his strength and ability, and it should have enough meaning to retain his interests without making such great personal demands that he will be driven away or that his performance will suffer. The appropriate social characteristics of a man-machine system can be investigated for any proposed system. They may range from isolation, which may cause performance to deteriorate, to so much social interaction that the task cannot be attended to properly. The social arrangements—workers unable to interact, workers free to interact, workers required to interact—can have a large effect on both performance and satisfaction of workers. The physical arrangement of the personal space of the workers and such environmental factors as noise, which may affect social interaction, can also have an impact on performance and satisfaction. All of the variations in physical and psychological requirements can be used as theoretical units to formulate theoretical statements. For example, "*Control design* is related to *perceived fatigue*," or "*Proximity to other workers* is related to *number of errors.*"

All of the technological decisions about task definitions are subject to continuous reevaluation. It is the nature of technological matters that the techniques of today are replaced tomorrow, and nothing is so naive as thinking that present methods will not change.

Work Force

The characteristics of the available work force are an important consideration in job definition decisions, but surprisingly, this aspect has not received a great deal of direct attention. The ability level of the work force has obvious implications for the skills required by the task. The expected education and experience of the available work force can be assessed before establishing or making changes in job definitions. Of course, the *education* and *experience* data will be helpful only if the relationships between those data and *performance* on various possible tasks are known. When the potential work force cannot be expected to have the necessary job skills, it may be possible to measure their trainability—that is, how much training would be necessary for the various job definitions.

Differences in skill levels are not the only work-force characteristics to be investigated, however. Here again, it is also useful to consider worker attitudes and the meaningfulness of the work. For example, there are cultural differences in the expectations which persons bring with them to the job. Job definitions which will optimize performance and satisfaction in a manufacturing plant differ greatly depending on whether the plant is to be the first manufacturing plant in a traditionally rural area of Idaho or one more manufacturing firm in urban Chicago. Workers from different communities differ in the amount of personal involvement they want in their jobs, the amount of risk they are willing to tolerate, the amount of routine and repetition they expect, and the kinds of desires which they expect to be fulfilled (financial, security, prestige, social, and so on). Careful investigation of the work force expectations may avoid the creation of tasks which will be seen as "bad" and which might be left when alternatives more closely approximating the workers' expectations appear.

Organization Policy

It was suggested previously that a third area of consideration, organization policies, might be important in making job definition decisions. That is to say that job definitions often are influenced by the policy makers' conjectures about what "ought" to be. Such conjectures are based on moral and philosophical grounds and must be considered because of the frequently sweeping impact that they have on the operation of organizations. The most important of these policies are opinions about the amount of discretion a worker should have in the performance of his task. Should the job definition be a general specification of goals, leaving the worker to choose his own procedures, or should performance methods be specified in careful detail from which the worker is not allowed to vary? The answers to this question are nearly as numerous as attempts to answer it. The actual answer for any particular job definition is likely to depend on the technology and work force of the specific job and the personal predispositions of the persons responsible for the job definition. There are few, if any, organizations which approach either end of the "worker discretion" continuum throughout the organization.

Job definition is an obvious problem for the new organization. For a continuing organization, it is a problem which demands regular reassessment. Whenever there are changes in relevant technology, work force characteristics, or company policy, there should be a corresponding consideration of job definition.

Job Analysis

We have examined job design and man-machine relationships. Job design considerations pertain to how a job or individual task *should* be performed. *Job analysis*, however, generally is concerned with studying and examining the various components of *existing* jobs; it provides a picture of the interrelationships among components in a specific job and among jobs in general. Job analysis yields a description of the way current employees are performing the job.

A job analysis occasionally may show that the task is not being performed according to the job design.

It should be noted that incumbents usually provide the bulk of information for job analyses. However, we are discussing this topic under "Developing the Organization" because the ultimate result of a job analysis is a picture of how the job is performed. Job analysis indicates the required duties, the conditions under which work is performed, the qualifications of the worker, and eventually provides a base from which to evaluate the actual behavior of a worker. Thus, the topic is appropriate to our present discussion. Another reason for discussing job analysis at this point is that the topics in the second section, "Obtaining Members," cannot be adequately covered without assuming job analysis information.

Specific Uses of Job Analysis

There are several specific uses of job analysis for large or small organizations. It has been thought that job analysis generally is appropriate only for large companies, which have a considerable number of individuals performing specific tasks. It is true that a large number of employees provides more accurate average pictures of jobs whereas job analysis in small companies provides unique patterns. But job analysis is valuable for all organizations. Organizational planning, which includes describing the responsibility, authority, and decision-making structure, is particularly appropriate for organizations, regardless of size. But analysis for personnel use may be of little value to small companies because an insufficient number of employees precludes empirical studies of selection procedures.

ORGANIZATIONAL PLANNING

Job analysis is essential from the general standpoint of organizational structure. First, it provides all members of the organization with information about the *authority structure*—who makes the decisions and who carries out the specific tasks. Second, and related to the authority structure, is information about *responsibility structure.* Employees will know to whom they are responsible, and managers, foremen, and supervisors will know how much responsibility they have. Third, job analysis provides information on *delimitation of functions.* That is, each employee knows what is expected of him, what he should and should not be doing, and how to do it. A job analysis for a shop foreman of ORG would indicate that he is responsible to a staff foreman, that his span of control gives him authority over seven or eight workers, and what tasks he is expected to perform.

These organizational planning uses facilitate the operation of the company. Conflicts between or within units are lessened, and the probability of duplication in decision making, enacting decisions, or work functions is diminished. Broader uses involve job design, which we have already discussed, and job evaluation. Job analysis provides information with respect to whether the job should be redesigned and with respect to the design of new but similar tasks. Job evaluation is concerned with wage and salary administration and is a function of the general difficulty of the job and worth of the worker. (Job evaluation will be covered in Chapter Seven.)

PERSONNEL USES

Without job analysis, *selection and placement* could not be properly administered. Before constructing or purchasing any test to be used for selection, a job analysis should be performed so that we know what the job entails before we try to predict success in the job. Job requirements and qualifications also are based on job analysis. This information prescribes which applicants we recruit and hire. Finally, the criterion aspect of selection (to be discussed in Chapter Four) is related to job analysis. Briefly, the criterion is the measure of success, and to measure success we have to know the components of the job, what is considered success with the component, and how to measure it.

Job analysis also is essential to *training and development*. Knowing the work and skills required for a job allows us to develop those training programs which are most likely to lead to successful learning of the job. Personnel development programs and promotions and transfer are also predicated on job analysis information. Promotion or transfer of workers from one job or level to another is more successful if common job components are identified. For example, job analyses might reveal that typist and keypunch tasks and requirements are similar. This facilitates the development of training programs which would allow transfer from one of these jobs to the other, or the job might be redesigned to include both typing and keypunch tasks.

Sources of Job Analysis Information

Several general methods of job analysis are discussed in the next section. Regardless of the method, however, one or more sources for information are utilized by the job analyst. A preliminary source is the *Dictionary of Occupational Titles* (DOT, 1965). The DOT is a two-volume *encyclopedic source* of information. Volume I alphabetically lists approximately 22,000 job titles and defines each in a paragraph. Each job has a six-digit code: the first digit indicates the major occupational category, the next two digits indicate subgroups within that category, and the last three digits indicate specific occupations within the subgroup. This code illustrates one of the values of job analysis—jobs can be categorized according to task similarities. Volume II lists all jobs numerically, according to their code number. For example, the following is the DOT job description of a job analyst in ORG or any other organization:

> Job Analyst (profess. & kin.) 166.088 occupational analyst.
>
> Collects, analyzes, and develops occupational data concerning jobs, job qualifications, and worker characteristics to facilitate personnel, administrative, or information functions in private, public, or governmental organizations: Consults with management to determine type, scope, and purpose of analyses, and compiles staffing schedules, flow charts, and other background information about company policies and facilities to expedite study. Studies jobs being performed and interviews workers and supervisory personnel to ascertain physical and mental requirements of jobs in relation to materials, products, procedures, subject matter, and services involved. Writes job description specifications, detailed analysis schedules, and narrative and statistical reports reflecting such data as physical demands, working conditions, skills, knowledges, abilities, training, education, and related factors required to perform jobs. Conducts related occupational research utilizing publications, professional and trade associations, and other media to verify or standardize data. Submits written reports pertaining to personnel job policies, morale, absenteeism, turnover, job breakdown and dilution, organization, staffing, and related items. Utilizes data to evolve or improve wage evaluation systems, counseling, and interviewing aids, training and testing programs, and other personnel practices. May write descriptions or monographs of jobs, processes, and industrial patterns or trends for publication. May be designated according to phase of analysis performed as Physical-Demands Analyst.

The group of jobs indexed by the number 166 includes such jobs as job analyst, personnel technician, wage classification specialist, and insurance and pension administrator.

Examination of the example indicates that the job is described briefly and generally. It offers a description of the average mode of performing the particular job, a synthesis of how the job is performed in various places under various conditions. However, the description provided by DOT is no substitute for doing the job analysis in a specific company. That is, the DOT description should not be generalized to a specific company; job analysis should be performed for specific jobs in specific companies. What is the effective purpose of the DOT? First, it acquaints a job analyst, who is not necessarily familiar with the specific job of interest, with the appropriate job terminology. Second, the job analyst gains insight into the general areas about which he should be gathering specific information.

Other sources which serve the same function are *previous job analyses* performed in the same company or even other companies in similar industries. Again, the indicated terminology and general areas of concern are useful. Also, comparing present and previous analyses can indicate the manner in which job functions or organizations have changed. Previous job analyses cannot be relied on alone, of course, because of such changes.

The basic sources for job analyses are the people directly involved, *incumbent workers* and *supervisory personnel*, and most job analysis methods require both workers and their supervisors to describe the job. Such *experts* as staff personnel and industrial and human engineers can also provide information. They may provide insights about which the job analyst and incumbents would not ordinarily be aware.

Methods of Job Analysis

CHECKLISTS

This procedure is used to collect information about a particular job and somewhat ignores its relationship and interaction with other jobs in the company. A long list of activities and working conditions usually is provided to the job analyst or other source, who indicates whether the item is relevant for the particular job or the degree or frequency with which the behavior expressed in the item appears.

Figure 3.1 shows some items in a checklist format which might be used in developing a job analysis. The job analyst simply records the frequency of occurrence of the activity for each job. The activities may be defined in considerable detail.

FREQUENCY OF OCCURRENCE

Activities	Never	Once per month	Once per week	Once per day	Once per hour	More than once per hour
Computing						
Consulting						
Copying						
Handling						
Manipulating						
Writing						

FIGURE 3.1. *A partial list of activities which might be included on a job analysis checklist.*

As already indicated, the checklist procedure does not provide an integrated analysis of the job situation. Also, if the items are general descriptions and not specific behaviors, the resulting picture of the job can be vague and inaccurate. The advantages to this procedure, which may not sufficiently compensate for the deficiencies, are ease in use, administration, and tabulation.

CRITICAL INCIDENTS

A critical incident procedure developed by Flanagan (1954) provides for the collection of behaviors which differentiate between successful and unsuccessful employees. A composite of these incidents describes the crucial aspects of the job. The advantages are that the collection of critical incidents requires information on the conditions prior to the critical behaviors, the exact nature of the behavior, and the consequences of the behavior. Also, actual behaviors are noted instead of general terms or opinions.

There are, however, two basic disadvantages. First, the identification of critical behaviors requires long periods of observation and recording. Second, and most important, a job analysis should indicate how the job should be performed by the average or general worker. The critical incident procedure could yield descriptions that define outstandingly good and outstandingly poor performance but ignore the behaviors of average performance. Examples of critical incidents for ORG salesmen might include "Transmits orders to corporate offices at the end of every work day" (good performance), and "Ignores customer complaints and does not pass them on to appropriate people" (bad performance).

OBSERVATIONS AND/OR PARTICIPATIONS

Either the checklist method or the critical incident technique can be done by observation. Observation generally is any technique which requires the job analyst to observe job incumbents performing their tasks. This can be done in an essay or paragraph description of the job and its interaction with other jobs, but the procedure is time consuming and costly. Observation periods should be random so that a biased picture of the job is not obtained. Observing various workers on different times and days yields the most accurate analysis.

The participation method requires the job analyst to perform the job in order to obtain first-hand information. It is obvious, however, that the procedure is costly, time consuming, and suitable only for those jobs which a job analyst can readily learn. After performing all aspects of the job, the job analyst writes an essay description.

There are several general problems associated with the participation or work observation method. The most important, particularly for the observation procedure, is that the job analyst must remain unobtrusive and not interfere with the normal functioning of the worker and work. Knowing that one is being observed often causes changes in performance and consequently distorts the analysis. Furthermore, only tasks which can be completed in a short time are appropriate for observation. An adequate sample of workers must be observed and analyzed, and an adequate sample of the repertoire of activities must be observed. In both observation and participation, the analyst must not record his own or the incumbent's idiosyncratic behavior but the general characteristics of the job. Neither is the observation technique very suitable for jobs primarily requiring mental abilities (computer programmer, chemist, lawyer, for example).

INTERVIEWS

Interviews allow us to overcome some of the problems of the observation/participation, critical incident, and checklist procedures. The job analyst can interview several people and ask questions which sample behavior appropriate to repetitive or nonrepetitive jobs and mental or physical jobs. In addition, anxiety and differences in motivation, which might confound analyses resulting from other methods, may be alleviated since the workers' participation and cooperation are solicited prior to and during the interview.

The major problem with interviewing is distortion. Exaggeration of function and importance are possible during the interview, and, unless the interviewer is familiar with the job, he might not ask the appropriate questions.

Successful interviewing, whether for job analysis or any other personnel function, is contingent upon several factors: (1) advance planning of the questions; (2) knowing what information is desired; and (3) gaining rapport with and the confidence of the interviewee. The latter suggestion is particularly important as the interviewee often perceives the interviewer as a hostile figure who has a different status in the company.

QUESTIONNAIRE

The questionnaire is an economical way of obtaining information often provided by interviews. A questionnaire could be in any of several formats from a checklist to general questions about aspects, conditions and interactions on the job. The questionnaire can be completed at the respondent's leisure, thus alleviating the pressures of interviewing.

A problem, however, is that it is difficult to expand and follow up responses obtained in questionnaires. The responses may be lacking in detail or even inappropriate for the question, but it is usually impossible to explore these in more detail. Unique ways of performing the job, which others should know about and possibly follow, would not be detected by the ordinary questionnaire. A second problem is that it is sometimes difficult to motivate the respondent.

Summary of Methods

As we have pointed out, each of the aforementioned methods has advantages and disadvantages. Hence, the best suggestion is to use a combination of methods to provide detailed information from which one can draw an integrated picture of the job functions. Using several methods allows us to adapt to the situation and worker and to obtain complete and accurate information. The Position Analysis Questionnaire developed by McCormick, Jeanneret, and Mecham

(1972) combines observation, interviewing, a check-list, and questionnaire. The results of these methods yield data for the following six areas:

1. Information input—where and how does the worker get the information that he uses in performing his job?
2. Mental processes—what reasoning, decision-making, planning, and information processing activities are involved in performing the job?
3. Work output—what physical activities does the worker perform and what tools or devices does he use?
4. Relationships with other persons—what relationships with other people are required in performing the job?
5. Job context—in what physical and social contexts is the work performed?
6. Other job characteristics—what activities, conditions, or characteristics other than those described above are relevant to the job?

Assembling Job Analysis Information

GENERAL INFORMATION

Information gathered in job analyses results in *job descriptions*. Typically, job analyses have focused on *what* the worker does or what is accomplished. Such information is referred to as *job-oriented* analysis. For example, we could describe the accountant in ORG as one who keeps data on the financial records of the company. On the other hand, recent analyses have pursued *worker-oriented* information which pertains to *how* the work is accomplished. We could describe the accountant as one who compiles, analyzes, and transforms data. The worker-oriented approach would facilitate general job analysis information techniques and would allow us to compare jobs and classify job families more easily. The best solution would be to combine the two types of information.

SPECIFIC INFORMATION

The end result of a job analysis is a complete, comprehensive *job description*. Table 3.1 indicates the type of information that is contained in a job description. Though seven different information categories are given in the table, any specific job description may include more or less information.

TABLE 3.1. *Information provided in job analysis.*

1. Job title	All titles, labels, classifications, and general describers; essential for classification and bookkeeping purposes.
2. Work performed	Activities, duties, and procedures; worker-oriented (how) information, job-oriented (what) information, and why the job is done; relationship between individual task components for achieving the ultimate purpose.
3. Skills involved	General and specific job knowledge; physical (strength, height, and so on) requirements and mental abilities (reasoning, judgment, and so on), including dexterity, versatility, and coordination of motor functions.
4. Physical environment	Temperature, humidity, lighting, ventilation, hazards.
5. Social environment	Size of the group, interaction or team activity necessary, decision-making and responsibility structure; age and sex characteristics of the group.
6. Conditions of employment	Time of work (number of days and hours, day or night shift); rest pauses; location of company or unit; wage and fringe benefits (a function of *job evaluation*).
7. Selection factors	Personal characteristics (*job specification*) such as experience, educational background, and relevant personal variables (for example, compulsiveness, reaction to stress, emotional stability); purpose is to define the population which should apply.

Limitations to Job Analysis

Most of this discussion has centered on analyses appropriate for positions in which a number of people work. One limitation of job analysis methods is the difficulty in analyzing tasks which require considerable mental activity. Such information can be gathered only through interviews and questionnaires. This limitation is very relevant to managerial and executive position analyses. A more significant limitation for analysis of managerial and executive positions is the small number of people involved. Such positions as product supervisor and unit manager in ORG would employ few individuals and exemplify this problem. If we analyze the position of marketing manager, the end result is a unique description of the person presently filling it and not necessarily the job in general. As a result, if the position becomes vacant, selecting someone for it is difficult. In the instances where job analyses can be performed—for example, by combining all managerial levels—the uniqueness of the positions requires that more discretion with respect to job performance be given to the occupants than is ordinarily true for job analyses at lower levels.

A final limitation pertains to the stability of required job behavior. Because organizations are constantly changing, job descriptions should be regularly updated through periodic review. Otherwise the job descriptions will contain information about how the job was performed in the past rather than about how it is presently performed. The usefulness of job analysis for the various organizational and personnel functions will be limited if there is not periodic review.

Summary

In this chapter we have considered how required individual tasks are formulated to achieve the organizational goals. Job design is concerned with identifying how tasks should be performed. Job analysis is concerned with how workers actually do the tasks. Periodic job analyses will dictate whether jobs should be redesigned. One of the important functions of job design and job analysis is in the development of procedures for obtaining members for the organization. This will be discussed in the next section.

References

Job Design

Chapanis, A. *Man-machine engineering*. Belmont, Calif.: Wadsworth, 1965.

Gilbreth, F. B., & Gilbreth, L. M. *Applied motion study*. New York: Macmillan, 1917.

McCormick, E. J. *Human factors engineering* (3rd ed.) New York: McGraw-Hill, 1970.

Taylor, F. W. *Principles of scientific management*. New York: Harper & Row, 1947.

Job Analysis

Fine, S. A. Functional job analysis. *Journal of Personnel and Industrial Relations*, 1955, **2**(1), 1–16.

Fine, S. A. A structure of worker functions. *Personnel Guidance Journal*, 1955, **34**, 66–73.

Flanagan, J. C. The critical incident technique. *Psychological Bulletin*, 1954, **51,** 327–358.

McCormick, E. J. Application of job analysis to indirect validity. *Personnel Psychology*, 1959, **12,** 402–413.

McCormick, E. J., Jeanneret, P. R., & Mecham, R. C. A study of job characteristics and job dimensions as based on the Position Analysis Questionnaire (PAQ). *Journal of Applied Psychology Monograph*, 1972, **56,** 347–368.

United States Employment Service, Dictionary of Occupational Titles, Vol. I, Definition of titles; Vol. II, Occupational classification and industry index (3rd ed.) Washington, D. C.: U. S. Government Printing Office, 1965.

section
two

Obtaining Members

chapter
four

Criteria

Having established an organization and divided its overall goals into individual tasks, there is an additional act before persons can be chosen to carry out these tasks. We must specify the *expected* accomplishments of the workers in each of the positions of the organization. In so doing we establish the *criteria* for each position. Criteria are the evaluative dimensions by which a worker's performance and contribution to the organization are judged.

A criterion for salesman performance in ORG might be the dollar volume of goods sold. A criterion for workers in the production units might be the number or quality of gadgets produced. Establishing criteria may be more difficult for some of the jobs in ORG than others. For example, it may be very difficult to decide on a criterion for the E. D. P. consultant or for the research and development personnel. Later in this chapter we will discuss ways to construct criteria for jobs which do not result in a countable product.

The bases for general criteria are established when the organizational goals are defined. That is, the organization must determine its overall purpose. The assessment of specific criteria permits the organization to determine whether it is successful. Each member in the organization can be assessed on the criteria appropriate for his job to determine his contribution. The assessment can be used several ways. First, the organization can provide feedback to the member so he will know how his performance is regarded. The feedback can serve as a motivator; it can identify areas in which he is strong and in which he needs improvement. Second, since one result of criteria assessment is identification of the relative effectiveness of the members—that is, we can determine the better and poorer members—the organization can use this information for a variety of personnel decisions: who should receive bonuses, promotions, training, or transfers, or who to lay off during slack periods. Third, criteria assessment is essential for the empirical development of selection systems. We cannot successfully identify measures which will predict the performance of applicants unless we have good measures of performance.

There is really little question of whether or not criteria measurements should be made or should affect personnel decisions. Judgments about worker performance are made constantly, and those judgments influence personnel decisions. The question, rather, is whether criteria measurements will be made formally and systematically and whether the workers will know the basis for judgments about their performance. If these judgments are left to the whims or arbitrary reactions of those responsible for assessment, they will be of little use to the workers or the assessors or the organization and they may lead to unfair personnel practices. Recent federal and state guidelines pertaining to employee selection decisions stipulate that whatever criteria are used they must represent major or critical work behaviors as revealed by careful job analyses.

Criterion Problems

Ultimate versus Actual Criterion

Ideally we would like to evaluate a worker's total contribution to the organization. We would like our measures to reflect everything which defines success on the job. This would include not only measures of productivity on the worker's specific task but, depending on the job, favorable or unfavorable effects of coworker relationships, consistency in attendance, effects of remarks to customers and others outside the organization, and so on. The important thing to realize is that a worker can contribute to an organization in many ways in addition to his assigned duties, and if we are to measure an *ultimate criterion*, we must include all of these contributions for the period of time the worker is with the organization.

Obviously, it is usually impossible to measure anything like the overall contribution of a worker. Even if it were possible, there is a sense in which the ultimate criterion cannot be measured until the worker has terminated his affiliation with the company. Length of tenure has its own benefits (and costs) to the organization, and these can be accounted only when the worker's ultimate tenure is known. The ultimate criterion is an abstract concept which is not measured.

The measurements used for performance evaluation purposes are called the *actual criteria*: productivity measures, evaluative judgments, attendance records, or any of the additional factors discussed later in this chapter. The defining characteristic of the actual criteria is that they form the basis for the appraisal of work performance. They are the empirical indicators for the theoretical unit of job performance.

The actual criteria are always a substitute for the unmeasurable ultimate criterion, the overall contributions of the worker to the organization. The actual criteria are those we measure as an indication of overall contribution. The translation of the concept of a worker's overall contribution into an actual measurement therefore involves compromises. How then do we determine the adequacy of the substitutes which we choose? The adequacy of criteria is established by three separate conditions, all of which must be met at least minimally. They are the reliability, relevancy, and practicality of the actual criteria.

Reliability

Criteria must be measured reliably. If they are not, there is no reason to attach meaning to our assessments. In its technical sense, reliability means that if we make the same measurement twice, we will get the same result both times. It indicates the consistency of the measurements. There are several traditional strategies which are used for estimating the reliability of measures, and estimates are necessary because the measures used by psychologists often seem to have been obtained with rubber yardsticks. Reliability estimates can be thought of as indications of the amount of stability in the measurements.

The most straightforward method for estimating reliability is called *test-retest*. It involves using the same measurement device at two different times on the same group of people and then computing the correlation coefficient between the two sets of measurements. If the same value is given on both occasions for each individual, the correlation coefficient will be 1.00. The first administration will indicate an ordering of the individuals with respect to the characteristic being measured. If the second administration indicates the same rank ordering and the same relative distances between scores, then, we obtain a correlation coefficient of 1.00. If there are changes in either the rank order or the relative distances between scores, the correlation coefficient is lowered.

Suppose we were interested in establishing the test-retest reliability of a criterion for worker performance in a production unit of ORG. Further suppose one actual criterion is the number of gadgets produced. One problem with test-retest reliability is that measures of numbers of gadgets produced can change from one measurement occasion to another either because the measurement method is unreliable or because worker performance changes. If we standardize the procedure for counting the number of gadgets produced and if the conditions in which they are produced (availability of resources, machine functioning, and so on) are controlled, a correlation coefficient of less than one indicates some degree of inconsistency in workers' performances. If another type of criterion measurement (such as subjective evaluation of quality) is used, a correlation coefficient of less than one could be a function of the same degree of worker inconsistency or a degree of inconsistency on the part of the people making the subjective evaluations.

If the time interval between the two measurements is short, we do not expect large fluctuations in individual performance. Thus, a low correlation is due to unreliability of the measurement procedure. If, on the other hand, the time interval is relatively long, performance could be expected to change, and unreliability could be due to both measurement procedure and behavior. The point is that both sources of unreliability must be considered in determining the adequacy of our criterion measure. If we cannot measure something reliably, we cannot predict it. And unless we know that unreliability is due to behavioral inconsistency (not measurement problems) we do not have a reliable criterion for personnel decisions or feedback to workers.

Another method for estimating reliability is called _split-half_. Developed to estimate the reliability of psychological tests, the split-half is simply the computation of the correlation coefficient between two halves of a single measurement instrument. This involves correlating individuals' scores on half the test items with their scores on the other half. Usually, however, even-numbered items are correlated with odd-numbered items rather than first-half with second-half. If the latter split were made, differences in scores might be influenced by fatigue, decreasing interest, and increasing difficulty of later items, but the even-odd split spreads such influences evenly in the two halves. A similar strategy is appropriate when estimating criterion reliability. For example, if sales performance is the actual criterion, using the first and last halves of the year may lower the reliability estimate because of seasonal fluctuations. A division into odd and even months (or weeks or days) assorts these influences into both of the halves that are being correlated.

One additional point must be considered in regard to the split-half method. It is a statistical fact that a measuring instrument becomes more reliable as it includes more individual measurements. A psychological test, for example, can be made more reliable by adding more items similar to the original set (providing that the new items are as reliable as the original items). With an actual criterion which is measured over time, then, measurements taken over a year are more reliable than the same measurements taken over six months (or monthly reports are more reliable than daily reports). This is an important point when making a split-half reliability estimate, for if the measures taken over a one-year period are split into halves, we are actually comparing performance for a period of six months with performance for another period of six months. This reliability estimate is statistically lower than the reliability estimate which would be obtained if we compared performance for 12 months with performance for another 12 months. To estimate the reliability of the measure over a whole year the split-half reliability estimate can be adjusted by the Spearman-Brown formula (McNemar, 1969).

An additional reliability estimation technique is the use of *parallel forms;* that is, forms measuring the same concept with different items. To be considered parallel, certain statistical conditions must be met (McNemar, 1969). This concept of parallel forms, which was developed in psychological testing, can be used in estimating the reliability of criteria. An example of an actual criterion whose reliability could be estimated by the use of parallel forms might be the accuracy of a typesetter's performance on two different pieces of work (considering the two pieces of work as parallel forms).

Closely related to the parallel forms estimate is *interrater reliability.* Ratings by superiors on specified performance dimensions are the actual criteria for many organizational positions. The reliability or agreement of the ratings can be estimated by correlating the ratings of two different raters for the same group of ratees. This can be done, of course, only if there are two persons with sufficient knowledge of the ratees to make the ratings. When this is possible, the two raters can be thought of as parallel forms.

Relevancy

Actual criteria must be *judged* relevant to the ultimate criterion. Though we can, and should, insist that the actual criteria be statistically reliable, the estimation of the relevancy of the actual criteria to the ultimate criterion is a matter of judgment, not statistical estimation. Of course, that does not mean that the actual criteria are arbitrarily or carelessly chosen. It does mean that we must always be aware of the subjectivity involved in our choice of actual criteria, and make every effort to base relevancy judgments not on personal biases but an understanding of the task performance being measured (job analyses).

The first source of irrelevancy in actual criteria is *contamination.* Contamination of an actual criterion is the measurement of performance characteristics not included in the ultimate criterion. Suppose the actual criterion used to determine the size of year-end bonuses for staff foremen in ORG is the subjective evaluation of the product supervisor. That is, at the end of the year the product supervisor exercises his own discretion in allotting bonuses of varying sizes to staff foremen. Now further suppose that we observe the size of bonuses and characteristics of the staff foremen, and we notice that the closer a foreman's work area is to the supervisor's office, the larger his bonus. Here we would suspect that the actual criterion (supervisor's evaluation) is contaminated (by proximity of foremen or by frequency of observation of foremen at work). It is possible that the closest foremen are the best performers, but a careful analysis of the situation would be in order.

An actual criterion need not be a subjective evaluation to be contaminated. If we used the dollar value of goods sold as an actual criterion for performance of ORG salesmen, the measure would likely include more information about the demographic nature of the salesman's territory than about the salesman's selling performance. The performance of a salesman in a middle- and upper-income suburban area should not be compared to the performance of a salesman in an urban ghetto without taking into account those influences which are unrelated to the salesman's ability. Though the organization may want to know the demographic information, it should not be allowed to contaminate the actual criteria for salesmen.

The second source of irrelevancy in actual criteria is *deficiency*. Deficiency exists when some important characteristics of the ultimate criterion are omitted. Thus, if the only actual criterion is a record of attendance, there would be no measurement of performance on the task. This might be satisfactory if the worker's job precluded possible variations in performance, but when task performance can vary, an attendance record alone is a deficient criterion measurement. An actual criterion measure of only a typist's speed would likewise be deficient, as accuracy is also an important part of performance. A thorough job analysis is a safeguard against deficient criteria.

Related to the concepts of contamination and deficiency and to the idea of relevant criteria is the notion that the actual criteria should discriminate, or distinguish, between good and poor members of the organization. To test the discriminating ability of the criteria leads one in a circle, however, for it is the criteria which operationally define good and poor membership. Recall that one purpose of criterion measurement is to identify relative performance levels. Thus, if a criterion is to be useful, we should get variability of performance.

We can check on the discriminability of a criterion measure by determining whether the variation relates to someone's notions about good and poor performers. We can get a supervisor in the organization to select out those workers whom he considers the best and the worst. These two groups can then be compared on the measure which is proposed as an actual criterion. It should be possible to discriminate between members of the two groups on the basis of the proposed actual criterion. If the discrimination is not possible (if members of both groups get the same scores on the proposed criterion), we cannot dismiss the proposed criterion as useless because the basis for the supervisor's groupings may be contaminated or deficient. And if the proposed actual criterion is the supervisor's ratings even this procedure would not be valid since the proposed actual criterion is being compared with another set of supervisor's ratings. Though a check for criterion discriminating ability may be informative, the amount of information conveyed by such a check will vary from situation to situation and will depend on the basis of the evaluations with which the proposed criterion is compared.

Practicality

Time, effort, and materials costs must be considered when choosing criteria measures. In a goal-oriented organization criteria are measured because the information will help the organization accomplish its purposes. Criteria measurement is an auxiliary, not primary, purpose of the organization, and all of the organization's resources are not available for making these measurements. Though we might be able to devise actual criteria which measure nearly all facets of performance, if they require that normal operations be halted for a month, they are not likely to be adopted. Most actual criteria will have some costs. The determination of how much cost can be incurred in time, effort, and materials to insure reliable and relevant criteria is usually, in the end, based on judgments of the relative worth of good criteria. Any criterion evaluation system which requires considerable cost and time in its development and use and interrupts the normal functions of the organization may be impractical. An alternative might be a less elaborate evaluation system which is also likely to be less relevant and reliable. Thus, any choice of an actual criterion must make concessions to the possible and the practical. These concessions cannot excuse the requirements for relevancy, but there is no doubt that practicality may compromise those requirements. The degree of compromise an organization can make is limited by both moral and legal considerations. Federal guidelines on selection testing require that criteria be reliable and relevant, and moral considerations require reliable and relevant assessments of employees if the assessments will be the basis for personnel decisions (feedback, promotions, transfers, and so on).

Influence of the Actual Criteria

It is to be expected that actual criteria measures will be obtrusive. That is, the act of making the measurement can change the thing being measured. If a worker knows that a particular criterion is being used to evaluate his performance and if he knows that a valued consequence (promotion, bonus) is contingent on the evaluation, he will adopt a performance strategy which he perceives will enable him to be successful on the criterion. Thus, use of dollar sales as an actual criterion for the determination of bonuses may increase the monetary amount of sales, whereas number of sales as an actual criterion may increase the number of transactions. If the organization identifies several criteria on which performance will be evaluated, it indicates to the workers that there are several ways to be successful in performance.

Single or Composite or Multiple Criteria?

An important decision which must be made (once it is decided that reliable, relevant, and practical criteria will be used in an organization) is the number of criteria measured in reference to a particular job. If more than one criterion is to be measured, how will the information from the multiple measurements be utilized? Before going on to a discussion of the various actual criteria which can be measured, we will briefly describe the three most common answers to this question.

SINGLE CRITERION

The simplest procedure for establishing an evaluation system is to choose a single measurement as an indication of task performance. Some single criterion measures which might be used for various jobs are dollar volume of sales, number of assemblies fabricated, attendance, number of parking violations cited, or superior's overall judgment. One single criterion is used for a given task, and single criterion assessments can differ from job to job.

It is usually easy to find objections, for reasons of contamination or deficiency, to almost any single criterion measure. Few jobs are so simple that their performance can be adequately assessed by a single index. One frequent single criterion measure is an "overall" rating of general performance by a superior.

If it is possible to develop or find an adequate single criterion measure, however, the utilization of the measure is straightforward. Persons with the highest assessments on the criterion are considered the best workers. If the person using the measure is unwilling to use it as a direct judgment of contribution to the organization, this may be an indication that the measure is inadequate. If the results of the assessments on a single criterion measure do not conform to the user's notions of who the best and poorest workers are, there is the possibility that the single criterion measure was not relevant or that more than one criterion measure should be used.

COMPOSITE CRITERION

A more elaborate way of establishing a work performance evaluation system measures several performance criteria and separately combines these separate measurements into a single score, the composite criterion. The most simple mathematical model for such a process depicts the criterion (C) as composed of a set of subcriteria (c's) which are added together:

$$C = a_1c_1 + a_2c_2 + \ldots + a_nc_n.$$

This formulation includes, for each of the subcriteria, weights (a's) which allow the various components to enter the formulation with greater or less influence. It is the determination of these weights which is the basis of most of the problems in the construction of a composite criterion. Before discussing some of the methods which can be used to determine weights, it will be helpful to point out some of their mathematical properties.

There are two properties of a single component score which determine its influence on the composite score (Ghiselli, 1964). The first is its variance. Scores with greater variance have greater influence. This is an easy concept to understand intuitively if we consider the extreme case in which we add two scores, one of which has no variance at all (all individuals have the same score). Imagine a composite criterion for the job of product supervisor made up of two subcriteria—a rating made by the production manager on a ten-point scale and a record of the number of hours spent in the plant. Now imagine that the production manager thinks that all of his product supervisors are equally excellent (or he wants to avoid his responsibility for making these judgments), so he gives each supervisor a rating of ten. The variance of the ratings is zero. But all supervisors do not spend the same number of hours at the plant; that is, there is variance on the subcriterion of number of hours. Therefore, the composite criterion score for a supervisor will equal his number of hours plus ten. When we look to see which supervisors have the highest composite criterion score, we actually see only who has spent the most hours. Since everyone got the same rating, it will have no influence at all on the relative positions of the product supervisors on the composite criterion.

If on the other hand, both measures had some variance their relative influence would be determined by their relative variance (as long as the subcriterion measures are uncorrelated). The relative sizes of the means of the two subcriteria do not determine their relative influence, so a variable with a relatively large mean but a relatively small variance would have little influence. Differential influence because of difference in variance is usually avoided by converting the subcriteria to some standard score. The usual conversion transforms each individual's subscores into z scores and results in a mean of 0 and a variance of 1 for each distribution. Though it is not necessary to have variables with equal means in order to equalize variable influence on the composite, it is customary to employ some transformation (such as to z scores) to equalize them.

The second property of a component score which determines its influence on the composite is its intercorrelations with the other components. The effect of correlations on the composite is such that the more strongly one component is related to the others, the greater is its influence on the composite. This may be seen intuitively by recognizing that a particular component has a direct effect on the composite through scores on that component itself and an indirect effect on the composite through its influence on other components. It is not possible to separate out the specific influences of each of the components, and when they are correlated their relative influence in the composite will always be partially unknown. This problem can be overcome by using subcriteria with equal intercorrelations or intercorrelations so low that they can be ignored. Intercorrelations among components are more often ignored than honored in the formation of composite scores, but they should not be ignored out of ignorance. They should be disregarded only if their effect on the relative influence of the subcriteria is deemed insufficient to require taking them into account.

Suppose we wished to construct a composite criterion for the salesmen in ORG. As our components we might choose (1) dollar-value of goods sold, (2) number of repeat customers, and (3) number of complaints (with reversed scoring). All of these components might need to be adjusted to take into account the saleman's territory. If a salesman does well on one of these subcriteria it does not mean that he will do well on the others. Low intercorrelations would indicate that this may in fact be the case.

Now let us return to the problem of weighting the subcriteria. There are several methods for determining differential subcriteria weights, and we will discuss some of the advantages and disadvantages of the major ones. To restate the problem as it now appears, we have several subcriteria which we wish to form into a composite criterion in the following fashion:

$$C = a_1 c_1 + a_2 c_2 + \ldots + a_n c_n.$$

We have transformed the subcriteria scores so that they have equal variances and we are willing to act as if the subcriteria are uncorrelated (either because we are ignoring the intercorrelations or have ascertained that they are negligible). In this ideal situation we wish to determine weights (a's) that will reflect the relative influence of the subcriteria on the composite criterion.

The first method which we will consider for determining subcriteria weights is *expert judgment.* Since the adequacy of a criterion is fundamentally judgmental, as noted earlier in this chapter, it is reasonable to turn to those who are in the best position to evaluate the job to determine the relative importance of its various facets. A pertinent question is, "Whose judgment should be used?" Those who have the greatest expertise about any given job are usually the incumbents, but those who know the most about what the organization expects from those workers and how they fit into the total organization are usually in a higher position in the organization. In different situations it may be appropriate to use one or the other of these sources or to use a combination of judgments from within and above the job. Whatever the source, the required judgments are, "What are the subcriteria for this job?" and "What is the relative importance of the subcriteria?"

The advantages of expert judgments are that they are easily ascertained and come from persons who know the job well. The disadvantages are that experts may disagree as to the relative importance of various performance aspects and the judgments may ignore the relative reliabilities of the components.

A second way of determining subcriteria weights is the use of some *statistical property* of the subcriteria. Several possibilities have been suggested. One proposal is to weight subcriteria proportional to their reliabilities. The basis for this proposal is that the greatest influence is given to those variables which have the highest reliability estimates. Another suggestion is that subcriteria be weighted proportional to their average correlations with other subcriteria. In the example pertaining to job criteria for ORG salesmen, there would be three intercorrelations among the subcriteria—(1) dollar value with repeat customers, (2) dollar value with complaints, and (3) repeat customers with complaints. The average correlation for each subcriterion with the others would be obtained by computing the average of the two correlations in which it is involved. Thus, for dollar value it would be the average of correlations (1) and (2); for repeat customers it would be the average of (1) and (3); and for complaints it would be the average of (2) and (3).

The argument for this proposal is that the measure that achieves the highest weight has most in common with the other subcriteria which define general job performance. A final statistical suggestion is that the subcriteria be weighted according to their predictability. That is, the greatest weights should be given to those facets of job performance which we can predict most successfully. Since we will be making decisions about persons based on predictions of performance, this proposal argues, we should use as indications of performance those elements which are most predictable. The strongest argument against all of these statistical suggestions is simply that they reflect mathematical properties of the subcriteria. It may be that none of the statistical properties of subcriteria will be related to their importance in job performance, and that is what the weights are meant to reflect.

A third way of determining weights is to establish a *dollar criterion* basis for each of the performance facets represented by a subcriterion. Every subcriterion must be converted to some form which represents its dollar value to the organization. The composite criterion is then a straightforward sum of the subcriteria values. If the subcriterion is "creation of customer goodwill" a way must be found to express each worker's contribution to the organization on this dimension in dollar value. Though this may be fairly easy for such subcriteria as number of gadgets sold or defective gadgets produced (given a negative weight), it will be more difficult to express in dollar value goodwill among fellow workers or willingness to perform nonroutine tasks. If the job is one which allows a conversion of each of the relevant subcriteria into dollar value, the composite can be expressed in a meaningful metric. The urge to express all contributions to the organization in terms of dollars should be avoided where the subcriteria cannot be expressed easily in dollar value and where dollar gain is not the sole purpose of the organization.

A final possible solution to the problem of weighting subcriteria is simply to give them all *equal weight*. Though on the surface this suggestion seems to ignore rather than solve the problem, there are some merits in its adoption. First, it is an easy strategy to carry out! All of the subcriteria are equally weighted by giving them equal variances and adding them together. No time or effort is spent getting expert judgments, computing statistical properties, or converting to dollar equivalents. Second, the composite criterion based on equal weights is usually highly related to a composite based on differential weighting. That relationship is lowered when there is a great disparity in different subcriteria weights. If the effort involved in getting differential weights produces a composite that is correlated .95 with a composite based on unweighted components, it may be reasonable to use the unweighted composite and avoid the extra trouble. If the subcriteria weights are something like .65, .72, and .51, there likely will be a very high correlation between weighted and unweighted composites. On the other hand, if the weights are of the order of .07, .82, and .39, the correlation would be lower.

MULTIPLE CRITERIA

Our final approach to performance evaluation is the retention and consideration of multiple criteria. That is, several facets of performance are measured and treated separately, rather than being combined. The case for dealing with multiple criteria rather than a composite criterion rests on the notion that performance is not unidimensional. For many jobs there is no single way to be successful. While product supervisor A in ORG may make valuable contributions to the organization through his ability to inspire his subordinates, product supervisor B may make an equal contribution by his useful suggestions in meetings, and a third product supervisor may contribute as much through public presentations of the organization's program.

Ghiselli (1956) has outlined three ways in which job performance can be multidimensional. The first, "static dimensionality," implies that at any point in time or for any given period of time an individual's work performance can be evaluated over several separate dimensions. The second, "dynamic dimensionality," suggests changes over time in the dimensions involved in performance. This situation might be exemplified by the performance of a salesman. In the beginning stages of his career his performance may be determined primarily by knowledge of the product and the organization. Later performance may be largely determined by his contacts, personality, and the confidence he has established in his customers. The third type of criteria multidimensionality is "individual dimensionality." As described (but not named) in the preceding paragraph, this is the condition in which individuals on the same job differ in the dimensions on which they make their major contributions. Static and dynamic dimensionality refer to the multidimensional nature of a single person's performance which can be seen at one time (static) or at more than one time (dynamic), and individual dimensionality refers to the multidimensional performance characteristics which can be compared between persons on a single job.

There are some advantages to assessing and treating multiple criteria independently. When a person earns a high score on a composite and this reflects a summary of his general performance, he has no way to know how he earned the score if only the composite is reported and kept. Was he consistently high on all of the subcriteria? Was his performance outstanding on one subcriterion and mediocre on the rest? Did he perform well on most subcriteria but fail miserably on a couple? Also, if performance is reported only in terms of composite criterion scores, persons with the same score must be treated similarly with respect to rewards, promotions, and so on even though they may exhibit quite different performance patterns. Likewise, if we are trying to predict performance on the job, treating two people with different patterns of behavior similarly because of their similar composite scores complicates the problem of finding and understanding predictors.

If multiple scores are reported, however, variations in performance patterns can be utilized in making personnel decisions. Criteria measurements provide important feedback on performance evaluations to the workers. If this information comes from a composite score the worker learns only how his work is evaluated, not why it is evaluated that way. The difference in composite and multiple performance feedback is the difference between the coach whose halftime message is, "Team, you're not doing well enough," and the coach whose halftime message is, "Roberts and Graham block more to the outside on the trap play; Miles make your cut three yards earlier on the curl pattern; and Strauss keep your head down and eyes on the ball when you kick."

Multiple criteria present a problem, however, if performance evaluation is being used to make a decision about workers. A single, not multidimensional, decision is made to lay workers off. Such a decision is difficult if it is based on multiple criteria measurements. It is appropriate, therefore, to form a composite for those situations in which it is required but to use individual component measurements when their detailed information will be more helpful. In the development of predictors, for instance (see next chapter), we are faced with a situation which requires a single decision about job applicants. We must hire or reject them. Instead of developing predictors of a single, composite criterion, however, we may develop separate predictors for each of our multiple criteria. Then for each applicant we have predictors for the several different performance aspects. If an applicant is predicted to do well on all criteria our decision is easily made. If the predictions are inconsistent (certain predictors indicate that he will do well on some dimensions and other predictors indicate that he will do poorly on the rest), we must use our judgment to combine them into an estimate of the applicant's overall contribution. Judgment enters the process, then, after data have been collected and specific performance aspects have been predicted.

Criterion Development

We have discussed the issue of ultimate and actual criteria and how to combine, if at all, criterion measures. Now our problem is to develop or construct specific measures—empirical indicators—to evaluate performance, a frequently used theoretical unit. We have generally used two types of criterion measures, objective indications of performance level and subjective appraisals of performance. *Objective measures* are quantifiable and countable; *performance appraisals* are judgments and relatively subjective.

Objective Measures

Objective measures are essentially operational definitions and empirical indicators of the behavioral components of work. These measures usually are obtained more easily for positions lower in the hierarchy—for example, the workers in the three production subunits of ORG. These measures also are obtained more easily and have more value for employees who work relatively independently or for relatively autonomous subunits because they are more directly influenced by individual performance. At higher levels, positions are less clearly defined and external factors have more influence on performance. We could get an objective measure of a manager's value or contribution, but how much of it would be based on his contribution and how much on the performance of others under his supervision would be unclear.

Two broad classifications of objective measures are *production data* and *personnel data.* Production data include output, quality, and trainability. *Output*, the amount of what gets produced, can be easily influenced by extraneous factors. Measures of production quantity are only usable if the worker has a direct influence over the amount produced. For instance, the number of gadgets produced in an assembly line operation is generally determined by the speed of the assembly line rather than the performance of the individual workers. Therefore, the number of gadgets is not a good performance indicator for that job. As an objective production measure, *quality*, or how well the worker performs, is indicated by number of errors, number of rejects, cost of reassembling rejects, number of complaints about the product, and similar assessments.

Trainability refers to speed of learning or the differences in proficiency before and after training. Speed of learning is an appropriate criterion measure for situations in which there is self-pacing or self-learning. An example is learning the background materials necessary to sell a product and information about the selling territory and major customers. This material would be learned by each new salesman at his own pace. On the other hand, learning speed is not appropriate for situations in which all employees are allotted the same period for learning a task. An example is a two-week classroom course for salesmen on technical product information. Before and after measures would better assess how much knowledge was gained from the training.

Personnel data are usually gathered from records and files on the employees. The most obvious measures are absenteeism, tenure (turnover), and accidents. There are, however, certain constraints with respect to each of these measures. The basic question with *absence* data is how absence is defined. If absenteeism is an indication of performance, each day off the job is a loss for the organization. But if absenteeism is used as a reflection of attitude, then consecutive days absent could count as one absence, since there is an implied relationship among absences. For example, a week of the flu could count as one absence, whereas five Fridays and/or Mondays for extended weekends could reflect the actual days away from production.

Tenure also has some constraints. Do we equate voluntary and involuntary or job-related and non-job-related reasons for leaving? Does turnover after one month represent the same loss as turnover after one year? The answers to these questions dictate the manner in which these data are treated. We would like to predict how long a person will stay with the organization when we assess applicants.

Therefore, tenure is used as a criterion primarily in studies to develop selection systems. If we ignore the reasons for leaving, our data and results may differ from those obtained if we investigate only people who left voluntarily. Finally, with respect to *accidents*, definition is extremely important. Is an accident lost time, seriousness of accident to employee, cost of damage to company, and so on? Again, these questions must be answered before accident records can be used as criterion measures.

Yet another personnel measure is *rate of advancement*. Number and frequency of promotions and percent increases in salary may reflect job performance. A straightforward way to assess managerial success, for example, is to examine the managerial level obtained while controlling for age (Ghiselli & Johnson, 1970). That is, we determine the average managerial level for a given age. Those a certain standard deviation above the mean are considered to be more successful than those the specified standard deviation below the mean. A 39-year-old production manager of ORG is more successful than a 39-year-old staff foreman.

As indicated, personnel data are usually gathered from employee records. In addition to inconsistencies in criteria definitions, a more serious problem is incomplete, unavailable, or unused records!

Performance Appraisals

Performance appraisals are a means for obtaining evaluations of employees, especially when objective data are difficult to obtain. *Superiors*, *subordinates*, *peers*, and any other person in a position to observe performance may evaluate workers. Employees usually are evaluated on behavioral dimensions that have been identified through job analyses or some other procedure. The dimensions should be clear and assessable, not glittering generalities. Each dimension should be relatively independent of the others and reliably measured. A checklist format might ask a rater to indicate whether a worker is "dependable," a term that might have a different meaning for each rater using the checklist. Items or statements on the checklist should be descriptive and specific ("This worker shows up when scheduled and on time," "This worker does not panic in a crisis situation," or "This worker completes all assigned tasks according to specifications").

We have already discussed reliability, which must be assessed for both objective and performance appraisal measures. Since performance appraisals involve relatively subjective evaluations, it is often more difficult to obtain high reliabilities for performance dimensions.

One framework for the analysis of performance appraisals is the *multitrait-multirater* approach (Lawler, 1967). The approach requires more than one rater and more than one dimension on which to evaluate employees. Several independent rater groups (for example, raters from different organization levels) allow us to assess the *convergent validity*, or rater agreement on evaluation. Several dimensions allow us to assess the relative degree of their independence— *discriminant validity*. In ORG, the product A supervisor, a staff foreman, and a shop foreman could evaluate other shop foremen (peers) on such traits as job knowledge, organizational ability, skill in human relationships, and cooperation.

Table 4.1 is an example of the way the data from such a study would be presented. The numbers in the table are correlation coefficients which indicate the strength of specified relationships. Convergent validity reflects agreement among raters in assessing dimensions of behavior. Convergent validity is demonstrated by the strength of correlations between the same dimensions as rated by different raters (the circled correlations in the table). Since all of the convergent validity correlations in Table 4.1 are high and positive we can conclude that there is convergent validity for these subjective performance dimensions. The convergent validity correlations between raters for the various dimensions range from .60 to .77. Thus, we can say that the supervisor, staff foreman, and shop foreman agree in their assessment of good and poor shop foremen with respect to each dimension.

Discriminant validity reflects the independence of the performance dimensions. Campbell and Fiske (1959) suggest three conditions necessary for demonstrating discriminant validity. First, discriminant validity exists if the correlation between raters for a dimension is higher than the correlation between that dimension and any other dimension which has neither dimension nor rater in common. This is illustrated in the dotted line triangles of the table. The supervisor and staff foreman agree (.65) on the dimension of job knowledge more than on the relationship between job knowledge and organizational ability, job knowledge and skill in human relationships, or job knowledge and cooperation. The same is true when supervisor-shop foreman (.68) and staff foreman-shop foreman (.60) ratings of job knowledge are compared. The job knowledge dimension therefore meets the first condition of discriminant validity.

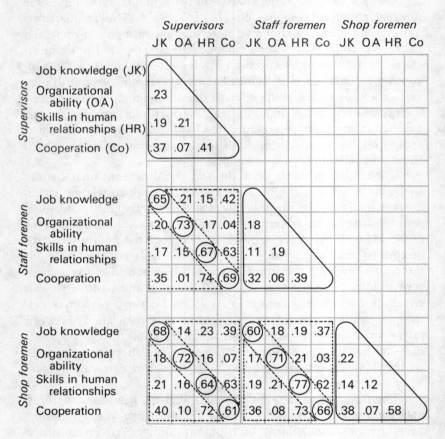

TABLE 4.1. *Multitrait-multirater matrix: Intercorrelations of subjective ratings of performance of shop foremen.*

By contrast, though the relationship between supervisor and staff foreman ratings on cooperation is high (.69), there is a yet higher correlation for these raters between cooperation and skill in human relationships. This is also true for the other rater combinations. This indicates that the staff foreman's assessments on cooperation correlate highly with the supervisor's ratings on skill in human relationships (.74). Thus, the dimension of cooperation does not meet the first condition of discriminant validity.

Second, a dimension should correlate more highly with an independent effort to measure the same dimension than with measures of different dimensions by the same rater. This can be seen in the solid line triangles of the table. The relationship between supervisor and staff foreman ratings on job knowledge (.65) is higher than any of the correlations between job knowledge and other dimensions rated by either the supervisor or staff foreman. An examination of the table will show that all of the dimensions for all rater combinations meet this second condition of discriminant validity.

Third, the same patterns of dimension intercorrelations should exist for all common and different rater combinations. This should be true in both the solid and dotted triangles of the table. Notice that in each triangle the lowest correlation is between organizational ability and cooperation and the highest is between skill in human relationships and cooperation. Since the pattern of intercorrelations is similar for all triangles we conclude that the third condition of discriminant validity is generally met.

Overall, then, the example data in Table 4.1 demonstrate convergent validity but do not entirely meet the conditions for discriminant validity. Different raters agree in their ratings of shop foremen on the four dimensions, but skill in human relationships and cooperation are not entirely distinguishable for this group of foremen.

Types of Performance Appraisal Forms

RATING SCALES

Rating scales are designed to assess the relative strengths and weaknesses of workers on various dimensions of job performance. The format used for these purposes can vary considerably (see Figure 4.1), particularly in the degree of structure provided to the rater. Some formats (c and h) provide more definition of response category than others (a, b, and e); rater response is easier to discern in some (e–i) than others (a–d); and some formats differ with respect to the degree to which the dimensions are defined (f and i are more defined than are the others).

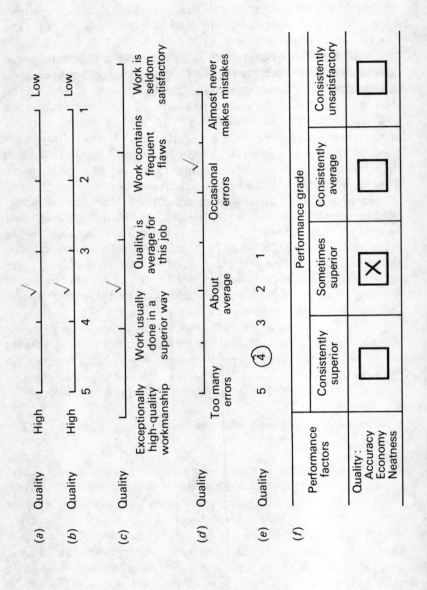

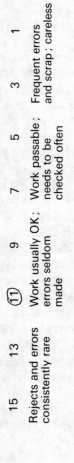

	1 2 3 4 5	6 7 8 9 10	11 12 13 14 15	16 17 18 19 20	21 22 23 24 25
(g) Quality	Poor	Below average	Average	Above average ⊠	Excellent

(h) Quality of Work

15   13   11   9   7   5   3   1

Rejects and errors   Work usually OK;   Work passable;   Frequent errors
consistently rare   errors seldom   needs to be   and scrap; careless
        made   checked often

(i) Quality of Work

Judge the amount of scrap; consider the
general care and accuracy of his work;
also consider inspection record.   20
Poor, 1–6; Average, 7–18; Good, 19–25.   ——

FIGURE 4.1. *Variations on a rating scale.* (From Guion, R. M., *Personnel testing.* Copyright 1965 by McGraw-Hill Book Company. Reprinted by permission.)

These formats are susceptible to weaknesses, errors, and biases. One bias, common to all performance appraisals, is *halo,* the tendency to evaluate the employee in the same way on all dimensions because of a general favorable or unfavorable impression. The amount of halo can be estimated by evaluating the discriminant validity in the multitrait-multirater approach. Halo bias would be demonstrated by large correlation coefficients in the solid triangles of Table 4.1 and would be one reason for a lack of discriminant validity.

Logical error, a related weakness, is the tendency of the evaluator to give similar ratings for dimensions that seem logically related. If dimensions are either glittering generalities or are unclear or undefined, it is relatively easy to make a logical error. Consider the performance dimensions of reliability and dependability. If the rater is to indicate the degree to which a worker is reliable and the degree to which he is dependable, it is possible that the evaluator will respond similarly because of the apparent similarity in meaning. If the dimensions were spelled out in more detail, however ("Dependability: The worker is always at the right place at the right time," and "Reliability: The worker can carry out all assigned tasks without direct supervision"), the rater is better able to see their independence.

Another weakness is *leniency,* the tendency to use the extreme ends (positive or negative) of the scale. This is a result of the rater's desire to indicate that the worker is good (or poor) in everything. If the rater uses himself as a referent, he may demonstrate *similarity* (evaluates others as he would himself) or *contrast errors* (evaluates others opposite to the way he perceives himself). *Central tendency error* is the rater's overly conservative and consistent use of the midpoint or average dimension values. Finally, *proximity* is the tendency to rate a worker similarly on traits that are adjacent on the form.

These weaknesses usually decrease the amount of information about the worker being rated. The most effective way to minimize such biases is to train raters and develop other formats. We must be certain, for example, that the rater is familiar with and sympathetic to the purpose of the rating. He should know why performance is being evaluated and how the results will be used. In addition, he should be trained in rating procedures (how to use the rating scale and how the dimensions are defined). And acquainting the rater with the aforementioned weaknesses may increase his awareness of the pitfalls in his task. Finally, the easiest way to encourage rater participation and cooperation is the use of meaningful and manageable scales. Such generalities as "He is a good worker" should be avoided as they are very susceptible to the biases mentioned. Behavioral descriptions help evaluate how well someone works and discourage general impressions. In other words, we should emphasize descriptive objectivity.

Likert type scales are the simplest approach; for each item the rater chooses one of five possible response categories (for example, a and b in Figure 4.1). The labels, or anchors, for the response categories are somewhat arbitrary but frequently include "always, often, sometimes, seldom, and never," or "strongly agree, agree, undecided, disagree, and strongly disagree." In either case, values of one through five are assigned along the response continuum and the overall evaluation is the sum of the weights of the response categories across all items.

Since the weights and labels are somewhat arbitrary, format alterations can alleviate some of the weaknesses we have mentioned. A careful descriptive definition of the dimension will help to avoid halo and logical biases. Omitting a midpoint on the scale (the "sometimes," "undecided," or "3") will reduce central tendency. And if more discriminations at the upper end of the dimension are desired, the values or weights can be adjusted accordingly. For example, in scale d of Figure 4.1, the midpoint of the dimension ("about average") is towards the lower end of the scale and permits more discriminations for above- than below-average performance.

CHECKLISTS

Checklists can avoid generalities if items pertaining to specific behaviors are used; the rater checks those items or statements which describe the worker's behavior. On *Thurstone type scales*, a behavior is included in the final scale only if it meets certain statistical constraints. Each potential behavioral item is analyzed by a group of judges or experts. An 11-point scale usually is used in the analysis, and the judge assigns a value ranging from 1 (negative evaluation) to 11 (positive evaluation), depending on the type of performance the item reflects. Means and standard deviations are computed for each item. The mean represents the scale value of the item; the standard deviation represents the degree of ambiguity or disagreement among judges with respect to the positiveness or negativeness of the behavior. The smaller the standard deviation, the less ambiguity. The items on the final scale cover the range of positive, negative, and neutral behaviors and each has a relatively small standard deviation. The rater checks off those items which describe the worker's behavior; the score is the *average* of the scale values of the checked items.

Figure 4.2 is an example of a checklist using Thurstone type items. Notice that the standard deviations from expert ratings are relatively small. The rated values of the items range from 1.8 to 10.5. If a shop foreman were to use this scale to evaluate one of his workers, he would check the items which describe the worker's performance. The performance evaluation score is the *average* of the values for the items which are checked. For example, if items 1, 2, 6, and 9 are checked, the worker's average score is 5.2 ([4.0 + 4.7 + 2.5 + 9.6]/4 = 5.2). Note that the worker is relatively low on such characteristics as quality (item number 1), punctuality (item number 2), and conscientiousness (item number 6), but he is evaluated as showing initiative (item number 9).

		MEAN	STANDARD DEVIATION
_____ 1.	Ten percent of this worker's gadgets are returned to be reassembled.	4.0	.92
_____ 2.	This worker is regularly 10 minutes late to start work.	4.7	1.10
_____ 3.	This worker completes assigned tasks without constant supervision.	6.2	.76
_____ 4.	This worker consistently produces more than the standard rate.	8.3	1.05
_____ 5.	This worker goes out of his way to help new workers adjust to the job.	7.4	1.25
_____ 6.	This worker stops working if the shop foreman is not present.	2.5	.50
_____ 7.	This worker distracts others from performing their tasks.	1.8	1.15
_____ 8.	This worker assumes responsibility in the absence of a shop foreman.	10.5	.81
_____ 9.	This worker suggests new processes.	9.6	.65
_____ 10.	This worker ignores suggestions for improvement.	5.1	1.30

FIGURE 4.2. *Performance evaluation checklist.*

Construction of the *forced choice* checklist also requires statistical analysis. Each item has a *discrimination index* (the degree to which the item distinguishes between poor and good workers) and a *preference* or *social desirability index* (the degree to which the item appears to be a "nice" description of behavior). The latter index is computed in a fashion similar to the Thurstone type item values (judges evaluate the items with respect to social desirability). Again, means and standard deviations are computed as a basis for retaining any item in the final scale. The discrimination index may be obtained by observing whether the item is used significantly more often to describe one group than another (for example, good or poor workers). The initial placement into groups of poor and good workers is based on a global assessment. Techniques for establishing discrimination indices can be found in discussions on test construction (see Wood, 1961).

The unique features of this particular technique are how the items are used and the task required of the evaluator. One version of forced choice requires the rater to choose the two items that are most descriptive of the worker. The choice is from a tetrad, however, or set of four items in which each has equal preference value but only two have discriminatory power. The other two items are neutral—that is, they are equally descriptive of good, average, and poor workers.

An example of a tetrad is given in Figure 4.3. All four items have similar Social Desirability Index scores. Only two of the items (number 2 and number 4) discriminate good workers; research has indicated that the other two (number 1 and number 3) are used equally often to describe good and poor workers. The forced choice rating scale consists of several such tetrads. Occasionally tetrads are composed of equally negative items, and the rater chooses the two which are least descriptive. The performance evaluation score is the *number of discriminating items* which are checked.

	DISCRIMINATION INDEX	SOCIAL DESIRABILITY INDEX
1. Completes assigned tasks without constant supervision.	+ .09	7.6
2. Cooperates with the shop foreman.	+ 2.63	7.9
3. Helps other workers.	+ .14	7.3
4. Checks his work before sending it on.	+ 2.75	7.5

FIGURE 4.3. *An example tetrad from a forced choice checklist for performance evaluation.*

The intended advantage of forced choice is to minimize central tendency or leniency errors. This advantage is achieved if the rater picks from a tetrad of relatively all good or relatively all poor items. A problem arises, however, because raters resist the format and spend more time trying to figure out the values than describing behavior. (The evaluators do not know the Discrimination Index values for the items.) Their full cooperation, which is required if ratings are to be successfully applied, therefore is not elicited.

The final and possibly best checklist procedure is the *behavioral expectations scales* (Smith & Kendall, 1963). This procedure involves the development of components, scales, and performance criteria by the groups who will use the scales. A group with work experience similar to the groups who will be doing the evaluations first defines the crucial aspects of the job. This step is essentially part of a job analysis and results in specification of the task components. The same group contributes critical behavioral incidents which reflect performance on the components. The most useful items describe behaviors actually observed. A second group then reallocates each incident to a component—that is, each group member examines each item and decides which component it measures. Those items most frequently reallocated to the appropriate component are retained for the next step. The reallocation procedure yields conceptually independent component scales. Examples of possible components are work knowledge, organizational ability, observational ability, conscientiousness, and human relations ability. Finally, another group assigns numerical values to each of the items which reflect the quality of the performance described in the item. Again, means and standard deviations are used to determine which items will be used in the final scale. Only items with small standard deviations are retained and subsequently worded as *expected* behaviors. For example, "Would expect this worker to recognize a defect on a gadget when the color is other than red," would be used rather than "This worker recognizes a defect on a gadget when the color is other than red." The expectation format facilitates the use of the scales. The rater uses the items as anchors and checks the value on the scale that describes the worker. Even if the worker has not exhibited some behaviors described in the scale items, the rater predicts the behavior he would expect given the behavior he has observed.

Figure 4.4 presents an example of one component scale developed from the procedures outlined above. The component title is Communications; the scale values are anchored by the items in the figure.

The scale is to be used to rate the communications performance of workers in a production unit of ORG.

Communications—the ability to present information clearly to co-workers

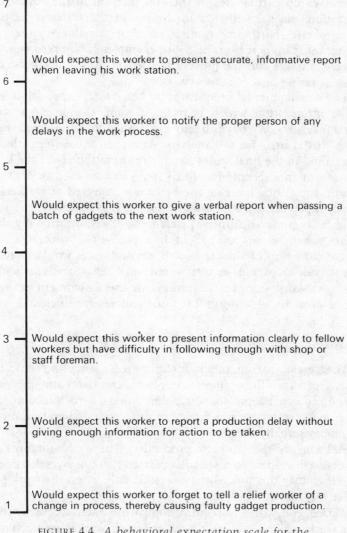

7

6 —   Would expect this worker to present accurate, informative report when leaving his work station.

5 —   Would expect this worker to notify the proper person of any delays in the work process.

Would expect this worker to give a verbal report when passing a batch of gadgets to the next work station.

4 —

3 —   Would expect this worker to present information clearly to fellow workers but have difficulty in following through with shop or staff foreman.

2 —   Would expect this worker to report a production delay without giving enough information for action to be taken.

1 —   Would expect this worker to forget to tell a relief worker of a change in process, thereby causing faulty gadget production.

FIGURE 4.4. *A behavioral expectation scale for the component of communications.*

One of the primary advantages of this procedure is that the rater group's terminology is maintained. The use of behavioral descriptions as anchors for the scale values increases the likelihood of agreement on the meaning of the scale values. The anchors on a typical rating scale, on the other hand, ("Agree," "Disagree," and so on) have different meanings for different raters. In addition, since the rater group participates in the construction of the scales, their cooperation and participation in the use of the scales is relatively easy to obtain. Furthermore, after checking a value on the scale, the rater must support his rating with examples of observed behavior. These advantages and the procedure itself minimize occurrences of the usual rating scale weaknesses.

The developmental procedures for behavioral expectation scales provide information which is useful beyond the development of criteria measures. We have already mentioned that scale items might form a partial basis for job analysis. And even those items that are not retained in the final scales provide information about the behaviors relevant to a specific job. Such items can be used in a training program, since they indicate the behaviors expected of workers. Because a supervisory group usually does the evaluations, the scales and items become an informal statement of organizational goals. If we also had the group being rated, in this case the workers, develop scales, comparison of worker and supervisor scales would enable us to identify discrepancies in anticipated work behaviors. Finally, those items with large standard deviations in the assignment of values indicate areas in which organizational policies are unclear.

WORKER COMPARISONS

Worker comparison methods eliminate leniency and central tendency errors since the evaluator simply differentiates among workers and indicates that some are better than others. This forced differentiation may create the appearance of differences where small or no differences actually exist.

Ranking is the simplest procedure. The evaluator ranks his workers with respect to a specific characteristic or overall effectiveness. Obviously this procedure is feasible only when the work group is relatively small.

Paired comparisons require comparing each worker with all other workers. The evaluator decides which worker of a given pair is better. This procedure is also limited by the number of workers;

the more workers, the more comparisons. (The number of pairs is $n(n - 1)/2$ where n is the number of workers evaluated.)

A final worker comparison technique is *forced distribution*, in which the evaluator places specified proportions of his workers into categories. There are usually five categories; 10 percent, 20 percent, 40 percent, 20 percent, and 10 percent of the workers are respectively categorized along a continuum ranging from good to poor.

Choice of Performance Appraisal Techniques

The appropriate performance appraisal technique will depend on several factors. The most significant, however, is the purpose of the appraisal. One purpose of criterion measurement is to assess differences among workers, identify successful workers, and consequently develop a selection system that will bring a higher percentage of successful workers to the organization. In this case, the choice of measurement technique depends on the organizational structure. If only one person is capable of doing the evaluations, a ranking or worker comparison procedure is easiest and quickest. If several evaluators are available, ratings and checklists are appropriate because they are suitable for other criterion measurement purposes and allow comparisons between evaluators.

If the purpose of the criterion measurement is to provide feedback to and motivate workers, a procedure should be used which provides detailed descriptions of performance on all important job components. Ratings and checklists provide descriptive information by identifying worker strengths and weaknesses. If this information is conveyed to the worker, it may motivate him to adapt his behavior. In fact, the information can be used in worker-supervisor discussions to determine the worker's objectives for the forthcoming year (a *management-by-objectives* approach). Since we know how the worker performs, we can establish future goals or objectives based on present performance. Management by objectives also allows us to consider individuals' abilities and goals when setting performance standards and expectations and to see if performance and outcomes match the stated organizational goals. Again, this information can be used to change the worker, the goals of the organization, or both.

Second, the choice of performance appraisal procedure depends on the evaluator's qualifications. His knowledge about his workers will determine the amount of detail we can request. The evaluator's level within the organizational hierarchy also influences his perspective on the worker. We should not be surprised to find discrepancies among supervisors', subordinates', and peers' evaluations of workers which may indicate differences in vantage point rather than inaccuracy.

Finally, if there is a danger of intentional or unintentional distortion in the evaluation, care should be taken to construct and use measurement techniques that eliminate bias. Regardless of its purpose, the criterion measure must be reliable, relevant, and practical.

Summary

We have considered one of the basic theoretical units in industrial-organizational research—performance—and the purposes and techniques of performance evaluation. We have also discussed the advantages and weaknesses of several empirical indicators of the theoretical unit of performance. This theoretical unit occurs in theoretical statements in conjunction with the other topics of this book; that is, performance can be related to organizational structure, job design, predictors of performance, job training, rewards, and job attitudes.

Recent legislation, court decisions, and federal guidelines have shifted the primary question from the morality of performance evaluation to the best evaluation procedure. The courts and federal agencies (Equal Employment Opportunity Commission and Office of Federal Contract Compliance) have emphasized that selection devices (predictors) must be established on reasonable measures of job performance. It is our opinion that a performance evaluation system that assesses multiple job behavior components with reliable, relevant, practical, and objective criteria and descriptive work performance appraisals will yield reasonable measures. In the next chapter we will examine the strategies available to demonstrate whether predictors are indeed related to performance measures.

References

Data Analysis and Methodology

Campbell, D. T., & Fiske, D. W. Convergent and discriminant validation by the multitrait-multimethod matrix. *Psychological Bulletin*, 1959, **56,** 81–105.

Ghiselli, E. E. *Theory of psychological measurement.* New York: McGraw-Hill, 1964.

Lawler, E. E. The multitrait-multirater approach to measuring managerial job performance. *Journal of Applied Psychology,* 1967, **51,** 369–381.

McNemar, Q. *Psychological statistics.* New York: Wiley, 1969.

Wood, D. A. *Test construction.* Columbus, Ohio: Chas. E. Merrill, 1961.

Criterion Problems

Dunnette, M. D. A note on the criterion. *Journal of Applied Psychology,* 1963, **47,** 251–254.

Ghiselli, E. E. Dimensional problems of criteria. *Journal of Applied Psychology,* 1956, **40,** 1–4.

Guion, R. M. Criterion measurement and personnel judgments. *Personnel Psychology,* 1961, **14,** 141–149.

Thorndike, R. L. *Personnel selection: Test and measurement techniques.* New York: Wiley, 1949.

Wallace, S. R. Criteria for what? *American Psychologist,* 1965, **20,** 411–417.

Weitz, J. Criteria for criteria. *American Psychologist,* 1961, **16,** 228–231.

Criterion Development

Berkshire, J. R., & Highland, R. W. Forced-choice performance rating—a methodological study. *Personnel Psychology,* 1953, **6,** 355–378.

Brogden, H. E., & Taylor, E. K. The dollar criterion—applying the cost accounting concept to criterion construction. *Personnel Psychology,* 1950, **3,** 133–154.

Fogli, L., Hulin, C. L., & Blood, M. R. Development of first level behavioral job criteria. *Journal of Applied Psychology,* 1971, **55,** 3–8.

Ghiselli, E. E., & Johnson, D. A. Need satisfaction, managerial success and organizational structure. *Personnel Psychology,* 1970, **23,** 569–576.

Smith, P. C., & Kendall, L. M. Retranslation of expectations: An approach to the construction of unambiguous anchors for rating scales. *Journal of Applied Psychology,* 1963, **47,** 149–155.

Zedeck, S., & Baker, H. T. Nursing performance as measured by behavioral expectation scales: A multitrait-multirater analysis. *Organizational Behavior and Human Performance,* 1972, **7,** 457–466.

General References

Dunnette, M. D. *Personnel selection and placement.* Belmont, Calif.: Wadsworth, 1966.

Guion, R. M. *Personnel testing.* New York: McGraw-Hill, 1965.

Maier, N. R. F. *The appraisal interview: Objectives, methods and skills.* New York: Wiley, 1958.

Whisler, T. C., & Harper, S. F. *Performance appraisal: Research and practice.* New York: Holt, Rinehart, & Winston, 1962.

chapter
five

Selection and Placement

Having established methods for defining the "jobs" of the organization in terms of the task performance which is expected of the workers, we can now turn to the central topic of this section, obtaining members for the organization. The chapter title refers to two ways of obtaining organization members. The procedures for matching persons to positions (or vice versa) are easily specifiable but they assume that we are able to measure job performance. *Selection* involves accepting or rejecting applicants for membership in the organization, usually for a specific job. The usual form of the problem would be 26 applicants for 18 openings for machine operators. How do we decide which to accept? Occasionally, a selection process is used to promote current members of the organization. *Placement* is more complex because it requires the matching of several persons to several jobs. Placement decisions usually involve persons who have been accepted into the organization. We must decide what function each should fulfill. It is necessary, then, to specify clearly the goals of the placement decision—maximizing production, maximizing worker satisfaction, minimizing interpersonal conflict, and so on. Since the selection problem is more often encountered than the placement problem, we will consider selection in greater detail.

Before discussing some of the procedures for regularizing selection and placement processes, one assumption of these procedures should be pointed out. The reader should consider carefully the implications and bear them in mind in any applied situation. Statistical procedures assume a measurable criterion which our selection decisions will maximize. Those persons will be chosen for each job who are predicted to perform best on the criterion for that job. The measure which is used as a criterion for the development of selection procedures can be any of the performance evaluation measures discussed in Chapter Four. It can be whatever we would like to maximize. There will be jobs for which we would like to choose those who are predicted to have the greatest tenure. In other situations it may be appropriate to choose individuals on the basis of their trainability. Whatever we choose as our criterion measure, there is an assumption in the statistical decision process that it is to be maximized.

In recent years, however, there have been challenges to this assumption. The recent presupposition is that selection decisions should be made on social grounds. Those persons are chosen who best accomplish some social purpose—usually increasing the representation of a minority population or disadvantaged persons in the work force. The intention of our point here is not to suggest that either of these purposes is wrong, or even that they are incompatible. Rather it is to make explicit the purpose of statistical procedures and to suggest that there are legitimate reasons to base our selections on other purposes.

Development of a General Selection System

In the following sections we discuss the considerations necessary to developing a general selection system. We begin by identifying the personnel needs of the organization. Then we present the selection techniques. Finally, we discuss how to evaluate the usefulness of our selection procedures.

Manpower Planning

A complete program of new-member acquisition begins with a plan for manpower utilization which includes much more than the specifications of current openings in the organization. The first step in the program is the specification of expected short-term and long-term manpower needs. Using information about expansion or reduction plans and usual turnover rates for various jobs, reasonable forecasts can be made about future work force deficiencies and surpluses.

Once we estimate future manpower conditions, policy decisions can be made and the consequences of various selection and training schemes considered. These considerations should include the costs of training, the costs of recruiting, the costs of a selection system, the benefits of transferring workers from one job to another, the benefits of promoting within the organization, and so on. From careful deliberation on these points it is often possible to plan career ladders or progressive paths for members. Thus members are encouraged to stay in the organization without being locked into dead-end positions. A possible career ladder for ORG may consist of hiring workers in a production unit with the intention of moving them up through the staff foreman position or into the salesman position.

Career ladders often imply that training will be carried out in the organization; that is, while at one step, members will be preparing for the next. A career-ladder strategy will mean that the most appropriate selection criterion will not necessarily be performance on the immediate task for which a person is hired. Selection procedures should instead consider how trainable the new members are and how readily they will adapt to later (probably more important) duties.

Though all forecasting is subject to error, intelligent planning can avoid shortages of persons with critical skills. Advance planning is the rule in administering production materials and facilities. The most important resource, manpower, should not be administered less thoughtfully.

Recruiting

The initial problem is to interest persons in becoming members. There are many ways to accomplish this—ads in newspapers and magazines, visits to college campuses, employment agencies, word of mouth, and so on. The technique should match the job available and the labor market. If an E.D.P. consultant is desired for ORG, an ad in a local newspaper will be less effective than a visit (or telephone call) to a college computer-science department. The methods of recruitment and publicity *do* influence the applicant population from which new members can be chosen. If one wishes, for example, to increase the number of applicants from minorities (or with high school degrees, sales experience, or money to invest), it is necessary to recruit in the locations and media which are most accessible to those special populations.

Recruitment costs should always be included in an assessment of the effectiveness of personnel policies. If qualified applicants regularly apply to the organization without solicitation, recruiting expenses are unnecessary. Because rare and valuable skills are more expensive to recruit, it is sometimes better to recruit and hire persons with lesser skills and to train them. There are few general rules for a ready-made recruiting policy, however, and policies usually should be tailored to the applicant population, the task, and the needs of the organization.

The characteristics of the applicant population are determined by the mode of recruitment, which in turn limits the appropriateness of the selection model and the information it provides for decision making in the specific situation. If the selection procedure is based on an applicant sample recruited in a specific manner, the results are appropriate only if succeeding applicants are recruited similarly.

Job Choice

Finally, before discussing the procedures of personnel selection, there is the matter of job choice. Job choice is personnel selection from the perspective of the potential employee rather than the organization. The selection problem is quite different from these two viewpoints. From the perspective of the organization, statistics can estimate the number (or percentage) of errors which will be made in the long run or over a large number of decisions ("How many of our 100 new production workers will perform at the minimum criterion level?"). For the individual, however, statistical methods estimate the risk involved in a single decision ("How likely is it that I will be successful if I take that job?").

Job choice has been discussed in terms of the developmental process of a personal career, the satisfaction of personal needs, and the grouping of persons with similar orientations in similar kinds of work (Crites, 1969; Holland, 1966; Roe, 1956; Super & Bohn, 1970). The two most popular instruments used in job counseling are the Kuder Preference Record (Kuder, 1960) and the Strong Vocational Interest Blank (Strong, 1966). It is not our intention to provide an introduction to the field of job choice; interested readers are encouraged to pursue the topic in the sources indicated above. All readers, however, are encouraged to recognize the difference in the individual and organizational approaches to selection problems and to understand that we deal here almost exclusively with the latter perspective. This does not imply that the individual perspective is less important, only that it is different.

Validity

Since we are concerned with hiring employees who will be successful in ORG, it is necessary to establish a selection system. Stage 1 in the development of our selection system requires job analyses (see Chapter Three) and then determination of what we will consider as "success" in ORG and how it will be measured (see Chapter Four).

Stage 2 requires formulating hypotheses which state the expected relationship between our criterion (criteria) and potential predictor(s). The results of hypotheses testing will be expressed by correlation coefficients. When correlation coefficients are used to show the relationship between predictors and criteria they are called validity coefficients. What information sources (tests, biographical information, and so on) can we use as possible predictors of the criteria? What information will reflect differences among the applicants? What information can be obtained from or about the applicant that is related to our criteria?

The initial formulation of these hypotheses is based on systematic job analyses, experience, information from other organizations with respect to the predictors they use, literature reviews, and "educated guesses." The latter are usually based on the *face validity* of the information source. That is, some sources, as judged from their items, questions, or content, "look as if" they are related to the criterion.

Our guesses, experience, and so on also may indicate that there are some abstract concepts related to the behavior we are trying to predict. If we have measures of these concepts, we can hypothesize that they will be potential predictors of the criterion behavior. For example, it has been assumed that general intelligence influences performance of many jobs. Before we can test the hypothesis that general intelligence is related to job performance, we must develop a measure of general intelligence. The ultimate assessment of whether, in fact, we have a measure of general intelligence is a judgmental decision inferred from research evidence that is accumulated over many studies. If our measure of general intelligence is related to concepts that we expect it to be related to *and* unrelated to concepts we expect it not to be related to, we may conclude that we have developed *construct validity* for our measure. This assessment can be accomplished by a multitrait-multimethod analysis, by factor analyses, or by establishing *convergent validity* and *discriminant validity* in a series of separate researches (Cronbach, 1970).

Even though the choice of our potential predictor is based on construct validity, we must test the relationship between the construct and the criterion empirically, just as we would empirically test the relationship between any other potential predictor (picked on the basis of experience, face validity, and so on) and the criterion.

Before we review the empirical validation, however, we should consider Stage 3 in our development of a selection system—possible information sources or predictors.

Information Sources

One of the most popular and frequently used sources of information is the *interview*. It is used primarily to obtain specific information about the applicant's character, personality, job knowledge, and attitude. If these aspects are assessed, weighted, or scored, the interview becomes a predictor which can and should be empirically validated. The interview also fulfills other functions. If it is the first step in the recruitment procedure (on the college campus, for example), it may serve a public relations function. The organization has an opportunity to "sell itself." Facts pertaining to the specific job, company policy, types of benefits, and so on can be presented to the interviewee. These facts should facilitate his decision as to whether he desires to pursue employment with the company. Initial interviews also serve a screening function. The organization can eliminate from further selection procedures applicants who have very little chance of being selected. If the interview is conducted after collecting other types of information, all predictor information may be combined to clarify and resolve any inconsistencies.

In some cases, the interviewer is required to examine all the data and make a decision to hire or reject. This decision-making is based on the *clinical prediction* selection model in which the decision maker uses an intuitive strategy to combine and evaluate information. Evidence indicates that clinical prediction is not as good as systematic empirical prediction (Meehl, 1954). Because clinical prediction is an individual intuitive strategy, it is almost impossible to generalize from one decision maker to another or even to generalize from one situation to another for the same decision maker.

As a screening or decision-making device, the primary concern of the interview is negative information. Evidence indicates that interviews are particularly attentive to negative facts or information about the applicant, and this information contributes most to the interviewer's assessment (Mayfield, 1964).

In general, the interview, as a decision-making device, is unreliable and not highly related to the criterion measure. The usefulness of the interview depends on its relative structure and the idiosyncrasies of the interviewer. If the interview is relatively unstructured, reliable assessments are unlikely. If one applicant were interviewed twice, different questions might be asked each time and, consequently, different information given and different decisions made. On the other hand, if the interview were highly structured and interviewers asked the same questions, reliability would be increased. The totally structured interview, however, can be replaced with a questionnaire which saves time and money though diminishing the opportunity to pursue and develop responses. One strategy, thus, is the semistructured interview: ask a few prepared questions, but allow time to discuss and pursue points as they develop.

The problem of idiosyncracy cannot be alleviated by adjusting the format of the interview. Evidence indicates that interviewers' decisions are influenced by their stereotypes of good applicants, by biases formed early in the interview, by negative information, personal appearance, information already available to the interviewer (application blank or test scores), and even impressions of preceding applicants (Webster, 1964). Experienced interviewers can control how much the interviewee talks. The reactions of the interviewer—leaning forward or backward in the chair, sighing, frowning, or smiling—will influence the interviewee and are particularly important since they affect the interviewee's motivation (which he wants to maximize to present a favorable impression).

All these characteristics of the interview situation tend to restrict its reliability. Interviews do have value, however, as a public relations function and, with respect to selection, interviews are valuable as preliminary screening, when it is impossible to develop relatively good empirical procedures (the small company or small applicant sample), and when traits *can* be better assessed by the interview than other means. One special use of the interview is that it permits us to obtain and use as a predictor specific information about the job applicant's knowledge. Such interviews, *oral trade tests*, consist of questions which are phrased in the language of the worker and job.

Another information source which is a potential predictor is the *biographical information blank* (BIB) or *application blank*. Biographical information or application blanks contain personal, demographic, and situational information: age, sex, address, marital status, number of dependents, military status, past work experience, and so on. (See Glennon, Albright, & Owens, 1966, for a comprehensive catalog of potential items.) In addition, attitudes, preferences, and interests are frequently assessed. From this information one can obtain a systematic picture of the applicant which indirectly reflects his personal and motivational characteristics. One assumption underlying the use of questions pertaining to past work experience is that they may be the best predictor of future performance. In essence, BIBs are measures of those personal characteristics which are least susceptible to faking.

The essential point, however, is that the items comprising the BIB can and should be weighted and scored for use as a predictor. The easiest way to construct a predictor from a BIB is to select discriminatory items—that is, those which distinguish between successful and nonsuccessful workers on the performance criterion. For example, if 85 percent of our successful workers have two or more dependents whereas only 15 percent of those with zero or one dependent are successful, we obviously should prefer an applicant with two or more dependents. (Hypotheses pertaining to responsibility, mobility, and so on might explain this relationship.) The end result of an individual BIB is a sum of weighted scores on all items which is used as a predictor. (For a detailed discussion of weighting application blanks, see Guion, 1965.)

If items are used for decision making without evidence that they are related to the criterion, there may be evidence of unfair, illegal discrimination. Also, since many of the items can be more personal than a request for the applicant's age, the problem of invasion of privacy is very real. If the item does not help you to make a decision, why ask it?

References often are requested on application blanks. The information obtained often concerns the applicant's responsibility and motivation. Scoring reference information is difficult and requires a subjective evaluation or weighting.

Usually, previous employers and personal friends are listed as references. The lack of value to the employer of the latter source is obvious; it is not difficult to find a friend who will say a few good things in your behalf. References from a former boss are more difficult to evaluate. Does he really know enough about the applicant to write about him; can he evaluate the abilities that are necessary for the new job and the applicant's talent in relation to them? Then there are more cynical concerns. Some bosses will write a "great" letter so that the applicant will get the job and the present boss will be rid of him. Also, from the point of view of the new organization, "If he's so good, why don't you try to keep him?" Perhaps the best way to use a reference is as a screening device with emphasis on negative information.

The most obvious predictors are *tests*. Achievement tests measure how well an individual can presently perform; aptitude tests measure his potential. Tests can be differentiated into paper-and-pencil or performance; speed (how much you can do in a given time) or power (how much do you know); or verbal or nonverbal.

Tests of intellectual ability can measure general intelligence, verbal ability, numerical ability, convergent and divergent reasoning, creativity, and so on; psychomotor skill tests will measure dexterity, eye-hand or -finger coordination, and so on. Personality and motivation tests also can be used. The *job sample* is a specific test which requires the applicant to demonstrate that he possesses the necessary skills by actually doing the tasks. The job sample test is a simulation; it is representative of the work actually performed on the job and includes all of the important aspects of performance. If the job involves computations on an adding machine, the test would require the applicant to make similar computations. (For a general discussion of tests and testing see Cronbach, 1970. For a discussion of available tests see Buros, 1972.)

Basic Validation Procedures

Stage 4 in the selection process involves the examination of the relationship between one or more information sources (predictors) and the criterion or criteria. Because the purpose of a selection system is to facilitate selection of an applicant for a position, it is essential that we emphasize here, as we did when discussing manpower analysis, that the recruiting sample not only restricts the degree of generalization possible but, in effect, dictates the validation model. Validity, generally speaking, is the degree to which one measure is related to another. In employment situations, validity reflects the degree to which a predictor or information source is related to performance on the job, the criterion.

One appropriate validation model involves *predictive validity*. The purpose of administering a predictor, or collecting information from an applicant, is to predict how that person will perform on the job. The process of examining the relationship between the predictor and subsequent performance, the criterion, is referred to as predictive validity or the follow-up method of validation.

An ideal predictive validity design would involve administration of a potential predictor (we will discuss multiple predictors below) to a group of applicants. Based on chance, lottery, or any other random procedure, but *not* on the basis of their predictor scores, these applicants would join the organization. Though this procedure would maximize the information from the predictive validity study, only rarely is an organization willing to hire randomly. In actual practice, applicants are chosen on the basis of the existing selection system which the investigators hope to improve upon. The problem with this procedure is that the validation sample (the applicants who are *hired*) will not include persons who are rejected by the current system. Since we may not know the validity of the current system, some of the applicants may be rejected unfairly or potentially excellent workers may be rejected. We could never discover this if the current selection system is used as a screening device to determine who is hired into the validation sample.

In the ideal or actual case, if we are trying to validate a job knowledge test as a predictor, we would administer the test to the applicants and file the results without using the test scores for decision making. The results are filed because we have no justification for using them; at this point, we do not know if the test is valid in this application. After the applicants who were hired (the validation sample) have been on the job for a specified length of time, performance measures are obtained. The relationship between the scores on the potential predictor and the performance measure is examined and indicates the potential usefulness of the predictor.

Examine this procedure closely. It involves investing time and money in a predictor which may eventually prove to have no relationship to the criterion. The information necessary to determine the validity of the predictor may not be obtained until a year later, and then there is no guarantee that it will be valid. In addition to the cost and time, there is reluctance to hire anyone without using a "mystical" test score. In other words, the most appropriate validation model in its purest form is not that which most organizations would be willing to apply.

An alternative to the predictive validity model is *concurrent validity*, or present-employee validation. Concurrent validity involves the administration of the predictor to a group of incumbent workers, simultaneously obtaining criterion measures on them. Criterion measures can be obtained the day following predictor administration, the same day, or even a day before.

Now recall the purpose of validation and our discussion of recruitment. We are concerned with hiring new workers. What happens if we apply what we know about the relationship between the predictor and criterion for the incumbent workers to a group of applicants? First, the motivation level differs for the two groups. Our present workers will be told that the test scores "do not count," that they are being used for research. If the predictor is "valid," the new applicants will be told that test scores will be used to decide whether or not they are hired. The different instructions will affect motivation which in turn will affect results. Second, present workers have the advantage of experience when they provide potential predictor information. Their scores might be substantially different from those they would have obtained as applicants. Many applicants lack job experience. Consequently, the incumbent's experience will influence predictor results and affect any generalization to an applicant group. Furthermore, since those individuals who had performed poorly would no longer be on the job, the range of the criterion scores would be restricted. This would influence (lower) the predictor-criterion relationship. Concurrent validity is not appropriate for most situations. Unfortunately, however, many industries employ the model because it gives instant results! Concurrent validity, because of the problems mentioned above, and contrary to popular belief, is not an estimate (over or under) of predictive validity!

Concurrent validity may be appropriate for validating job sample tests, however. When we use job sample tests, we are concerned with whether the applicant can do the job *now*, today. That is, can the applicant type, operate the machine, and so on. Through a careful job analysis we would identify the important components of the job and how they are performed. We should attempt to validate a job sample test empirically. The concurrent validation model can be used to determine successful incumbents' performance level which, in turn, gives us a job sample standard for applicants. However, the predictive validation model again may be more appropriate. Because of organizational, situational, and personal characteristics, how someone *can* do the job may differ from how he *will* do the job.

Content validity is another alternative validation procedure, one which does not involve statistical relationships. Content validity is based on the judgment of the developer (a professional tester trained in the area of test construction) of the predictor measure. But it is important to distinguish between content and face validity. Content validity is established by a judgment that *the predictor is job-related*. Face validity means that *the predictor seems appropriate to the person being tested*. Though face validity may be useful in obtaining cooperation with the testing procedure or in convincing organization officials that the test is appropriate, it is not a sufficient (or necessary) condition for using a test as a predictor.

The judgment of content validity should be based on a careful and detailed analysis of the criterion which is to be predicted. This analysis will be either a total job analysis or, in the case of preparing predictors for part of a set of multiple criteria, an analysis of those job elements to be predicted. The developer of the predictor then constructs a test which will (in his judgment) representatively sample the skills, attitudes, or behaviors required by the job.

Content validity, therefore, is no better (or worse) than the trained judgment of the test builder. In some cases a predictive validity study may be appropriate for a predictor which has content validity. However, content validity frequently must be used if a predictive validity study is unfeasible: (1) there may be too few applicants to carry out the statistical analyses of predictive validity; (2) time constraints may prohibit waiting for the establishment of criteria performance levels; or (3) the job may be so critical or the consequences of poor performance so severe that one would not want to risk using the wide-range performance criteria required to establish predictive validity.

Results of Validation

We have mentioned *results of validation*. Whether predictive or concurrent validations, these results usually are correlation coefficients that are interpreted as *validity coefficients*. The validity coefficient r_{CP} ranges from -1.00 to $+1.00$, where the absolute value indicates the strength of relationship between the criterion (C) and the predictor (P), and the sign indicates the direction of the relationship. The coefficient can be tested for statistical significance.

Several precautions must be observed when interpreting a validity coefficient. First, most correlation statistics are appropriate for linear relationships between the predictor and criterion. If a nonlinear relationship exists, the traditional Pearson correlation coefficient will provide an underestimation of validity.

Second, if we do not have the full range of possible scores on either the predictor or criterion, again we will get an underestimate of validity. This restriction of range might occur in concurrent validation with current workers, who are likely to be relatively successful, whereas those who were unsuccessful would no longer be with the organization. Consequently, we do not have the full range of possible scores on the criterion. Restriction of range on the potential predictor may occur in the predictive validation model if applicants are hired on a nonrandom basis. This may decrease the range of the potential predictor in the validation sample.

Third, reliability of both the predictor and criterion limit validity. If the predictor and/or criterion is unreliable and therefore inconsistent in assessing its own characteristic, we cannot expect one to measure the other. Thus, if we have poor reliabilities in the predictor and/or criterion we will get underestimates of validity. We can correct for this attenuation and obtain an estimate of validity that is based on the assumption of perfect reliabilities (see Guion, 1965, pp. 31–33). This estimate will indicate whether it is advantageous to improve upon the reliability of the predictor and/or criterion.

In addition to a validity coefficient, we also obtain a regression or prediction equation. The regression equation, in the form of $C' = a + bP$ (where P is the predictor score, a and b are statistical weights, and C' is a predicted criterion score), is that which we use to make predictions for individual applicants. This equation and the validity coefficient are computed on the data from our validity sample. The data are the predictor score and criterion score for each member of the validity sample. If we are satisfied with the strength of the validity coefficient and decide to use the predictor in selection, we administer the predictor to a new applicant. We can obtain the predicted criterion score, C', for the new applicant by substituting his score on the predictor in the regression equation. Suppose the regression equation developed on our validity sample is $C' = 10 + 2P$. If an applicant scores 40 on the predictor his predicted criterion or performance level would be 90 ($C' = 10 + 2(40)$). Another applicant with a predictor score of 33 would have a predicted criterion score of 76. We would use this information in selection decisions by hiring the applicants with the highest scores or by hiring all who score above a specified level. (See Ghiselli, 1964, for a detailed discussion of the statistics involved in validation and reliability.)

The results of validation also may be expressed in *expectancy charts* and *tables*. Expectancy charts express results in terms of probabilities. The *individual expectancy* chart (Figure 5.1) indicates the probabilities of applicant success on the criterion given their predictor score ranges. For example, if an applicant scores 18 on the predictor, he has a 63 percent chance of being successful on the criterion. The *institutional expectancy* chart (Figure 5.2) indicates to the organization the percentage of those selected who will be successful on the criterion, given that the organization selects certain percentages of the best "scores" on the predictor. For example, if the organization selects the top 40 percent scorers on the predictor, 78 percent of these will be successful on the criterion. (Procedures to construct these charts are described in Guion, 1965.)

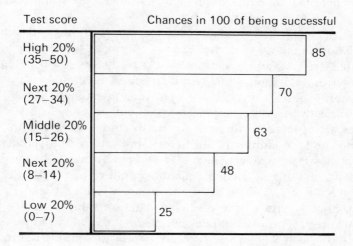

FIGURE 5.1. *Individual expectancy chart.*

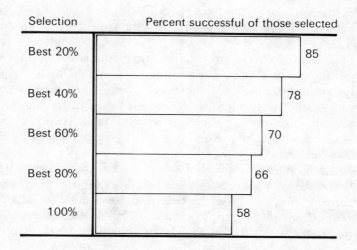

FIGURE 5.2. *Institutional expectancy chart.*

Extension of the Basic Validation Procedure: Multiple Prediction and Multiple Cutoff

To this point, our discussion of validity has been restricted to the situation with one predictor and one criterion. However, as already indicated, there are several sources of predictor information. Using more than one type of predictor can increase our understanding and ability to predict the criterion.

With one predictor and one criterion, we are dealing with simple correlation (validity), r. If we decide to form a "test battery"—for example, use a BIB and an aptitude test as predictors—we can employ a model of validation which simultaneously uses more than one predictor. Multiple correlation, R, provides an estimate of the relationship between the criterion and the composite of, in this case, two predictor scores. If the aptitude test is correlated $+.30$ with the criterion and the addition of BIB "scores" indicates a multiple correlation of $+.40$, we may conclude that two predictors are better than one. The resulting prediction equation would be of the form $C' = a + b_1P_1 + b_2P_2$ (where a, b_1 and b_2 are weights, P_1 and P_2 are two predictors, and C' the predicted criterion value). Suppose the multiple regression equation developed on our validity sample is $C' = 5 + 3 P_1 + 1.5 P_2$ (where P_1 and P_2 represent aptitude test scores and BIB scores, respectively). If an applicant scores 40 on the aptitude test and 6 on the BIB, his predicted criterion would be 134 ($C' = 5 + 3(40) + 1.5(6)$). Another applicant with an aptitude test score of 30 and a BIB score of 26 would also have a predicted criterion of 134.

The essential characteristic of multiple correlation is the composite of the two predictors; it is possible for one predictor to compensate for another. That is, a deficiency or low score by the second applicant on the aptitude test was overcome by his high score (favorable responses) on the BIB. The combination of the two predictors and its relationship to the criterion is the essence of a *compensatory model of validation*.

Generally, multiple correlation will be an improvement upon simple correlation if one of two conditions pertaining to predictor intercorrelation is met. First, the two predictors should be relatively uncorrelated or independent of each other while each is correlated to some degree with the criterion. In this condition, each predictor makes a relatively independent contribution to criterion prediction because the criterion is a complex behavior and many things contribute to success on it. Second, two predictors can be highly (but not perfectly) related to each other while P_1 is related to a degree to the criterion and P_2 is relatively independent of the criterion. In this case, P_2 is a *suppressor variable*. Suppressor variables operate to remove unwanted or noncriteria-related effects of the other predictor (P_1) on the criterion. For example, if we use a paper-and-pencil aptitude test of mechanical ability (P_1) as a predictor of subsequent mechanical performance, the relationship between this predictor and criterion is influenced, in part, by the ability of the applicant to understand instructions or questions on the paper-and-pencil test. Suppose that we have also obtained a measure of reading comprehension (P_2) from the validity sample and we find the following pattern of correlation coefficients: mechanical ability scores are highly related to reading comprehension scores ($r_{P_1P_2} = .70$); mechanical ability scores have a low relationship to mechanical performance scores ($r_{P_1C} = .25$); and reading comprehension is relatively unrelated to mechanical performance scores ($r_{P_2C} = .10$). Though the simple correlation between the mechanical ability test and mechanical performance is only .25, the addition of the reading comprehension test into a multiple correlation model would provide a multiple correlation coefficient of .37. Thus, the measure of reading comprehension serves as a suppressor variable. It takes into account the statistical effects of the latter ability and gives us a better indication of the real relationship of mechanical aptitude to mechanical performance.

Another possible way to improve correlation between a criterion and a battery of predictors is the *moderator variable* approaches (Zedeck, 1971). A moderator variable improves prediction by identifying the subsamples within a total sample for which the predictor is more valid. If the validity coefficient for a predictor and criterion changes with change in a third independent variable, we have a moderator effect. For example, if we are using intelligence test scores as a predictor of performance, we might find that the relationship between intelligence and performance is a function of job tenure. We could find that intelligence is related to performance for relatively new workers but that the relationship becomes weaker for those who have been on the job for a longer time. Job tenure acts as a moderator if evidence indicates that it is relatively unrelated to intelligence or performance in a given job.

An alternative to multiple correlation, or the compensatory model, is a *multiple cutoff* approach. Rather than permitting high scores on one predictor to compensate for low scores on another, the multiple cutoff model requires that a minimum score be obtained on *each* valid predictor. All predictor information is crucial; all characteristics, abilities, and so on are considered essential for successful performance. A decision to hire an applicant is made only if he scores at or above the cutoff on all predictors.

Two points should be made about multiple predictors. First, our examples have been restricted to two predictors. If three or more are used in either the compensatory or cutoff model, nothing changes conceptually (only more computer time is required); it is just an extension of the one or two predictor cases. Second, we have referred to the relationship between two predictors and one criterion. We do not mean to suggest that prediction of one criterion is an adequate basis for suitable selection systems. When more than one criterion is used, a battery or set of predictors is validated independently for each criterion.

Cross-Validation

In the discussion on validity, we have implied that if we have (for example) 100 applicants for a job, we administer a set of predictors to all applicants, hire all applicants, and finally evaluate their performance. We then compute a multiple correlation and prediction equation which is evaluated for statistical significance; if the significance is satisfactory, we subsequently use the predictors for selection decisions on new applicant samples.

This validation procedure is not complete. If we employ the procedure as described, there is the problem that the statistical results (prediction weights—a's and b's) may be biased or distorted due to capitalization on chance factors in that specific sample of 100. The regression equation may be unique to that specific validity sample and would not be useful in new but similar applicant samples. Consequently, it is necessary to *cross-validate*, or determine how effective the prediction equation is. We need to know whether the same equation would occur in similar samples.

Cross-validation usually involves splitting the *total initial sample* (100) into two subsamples (subsample sizes are arbitrary). The regression equation is computed for one subsample ($N = 67$) and then applied to the other subsample, the hold-out group ($N = 33$). For this *first subsample*, we might obtain an equation such as $C' = 6 + 4P_1 + 3P_2$. If the predictor scores for the *holdout* group are substituted in this equation, we obtain a *predicted criterion score* for each member of the holdout group. However, we do know the *actual* criterion scores for the members of the hold-out group. The correlation between the predicted and the actual scores for the hold-out subsample is an indication of the *validity of the predictor battery.* If this coefficient is statistically significant, the prediction equation is potentially useful.

There is, however, a dilemma to cross-validation. By splitting the total sample into two subgroups we obtain an unbiased estimate of predictor validity for future samples. But the subsample regression equation itself is more likely to be in error than one based on a larger, total sample. Several researchers have investigated this dilemma (Campbell, 1967; Chandler, 1964; Gollob, 1967, 1968; Mosier, 1951; Norman, 1965), but there is no statistically satisfactory resolution.

We should emphasize that cross-validation is not independent of or in addition to the validity procedure previously described. Validation involves cross-validation; it is a simultaneous procedure. Validity results that do not include cross-validation should be regarded with caution.

Utility of Selection Systems

Cross-validation provides evidence of the *statistical* significance of prediction equations. Another consideration is *practical* significance, or utility, which is Stage 5 in our validation procedure. Does a valid selection system result in the hiring of a percentage of workers who will eventually be considered successful greater than the percentage of successful workers hired without the selection system? The basic parameter in a discussion of utility is the decision maker's value judgment in relation to the relative worth of various decision results, payoff matrices. These value judgments or statements are difficult to measure. The basic strategy is to maximize the average gain for the organization in obtaining satisfactory workers. The preferred selection strategy is that which provides the greatest gain or utility value. In evaluating the strategies, we consider the gain in hiring with a selection system as opposed to no selection system, one system as opposed to another, and cost and time of systematic selection. With respect to costs, we are concerned with recruiting, training, and material costs and costs due to incorrect decisions. If the company hires someone who turns out to be unsuccessful, the costs are obvious. However, we must consider the other possibility—the costs of rejecting someone who would have been successful. Not only does the organization lose, but the effects on the applicant may be severe. (See Cronbach & Gleser, 1965, for a discussion of utility in terms of decision theory.)

The simplest way to evaluate the utility of a selection system is to examine a scatterplot (Figure 5.3). The data used to form the scatterplot are obtained from the members of the validity sample.

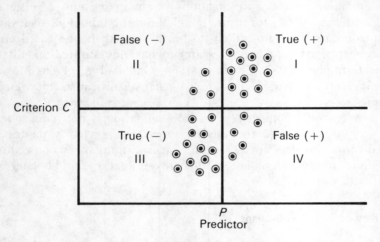

FIGURE 5.3. *Scatterplot of criterion and predictor data.*

Suppose Score *C* on the criterion is the point dividing successful and unsuccessful workers. Suppose, also, that score *P* on the predictor is the cut-off point that determines who is hired and rejected. This point can be determined so that the least number of errors is made—that is, the fewest number of unsuccessful workers would be hired and the fewest number of successful workers would be rejected. Unless the validity coefficient is one, there will be errors. Separating the group at P and C on the predictor and criterion respectively results in the division of the scatterplot into quadrants.

Quadrants I and III reveal the number of workers correctly identified, as either successful (*true positive*) or unsuccessful (*true negative*). Quadrant II indicates the number of workers that the test indicates will do poorly (because they score below P) but who are evaluated eventually as successful (the *false negatives*). Quadrant IV indicates the number of workers who would be hired on the basis of their predictor score but who are subsequently evaluated as unsuccessful (the *false positives*).

To determine if the selection system is useful, the percentage of workers who would be considered successful if chosen on the basis of the selection system can be compared with the percentage considered successful and chosen without systematic predictor information. The latter percentage is the *base rate*. The base rate is determined by the ratio

$$\frac{I + II}{I + II + III + IV.}$$

To determine the gain or percentage increase in successful workers if a new selection system is used, we can use the formula

$$\frac{I}{I + IV} - \frac{I + II}{I + II + III + IV.}$$

The first part of the formula indicates the percentage of workers who are hired on the basis of the selection system and who are considered successful on the criterion. The second part of the formula is the base rate. The difference is the percentage improvement, or gain.

Taylor-Russell tables (1939) present the gain in using a selection system where a new predictor is added to existing selection procedures. The gain depends on validity coefficients, base rates, and selection ratios. The selection ratio is the number of people to be hired, divided by the number of applicants. If the validity coefficient and the base rate are held constant as the selection ratio is increased (the greater the percentage of people hired), the gain will decrease. If the validity coefficient and selection ratio are held constant, the greater the base rate, the less the gain. If the base rate and the selection ratio are held constant, as the validity coefficient increases so does the gain.

The Naylor-Shine (1965) tables also assess utility, but based on different information. These tables indicate improvement in selection based on validity coefficients, selection ratios, and specified predictor cut-off scores. If a certain criterion level is desired, we can determine what selection ratio should be applied for given validity coefficients and predictor cut-off scores.

Reevaluation

Stage 6, the final stage in validation, requires that validity coefficients be reassessed periodically. We have already pointed out, in

Chapter Four, that criteria and performance are dynamic. The job itself, the way tasks are performed, and the characteristics of the people performing the tasks change over time; thus, we also should expect validity coefficients to change. If we continuously use a predictor or set of predictors, we should regularly check the validity for any changes.

Synthetic Validity

The validation procedure described above is appropriate when at least 50 to 60 people are employed in one job and many people are hired for it—that is, correlational analyses are feasible. Many organizations, however, do not have 60 people in the entire hierarchy, from part-time stockboy to president. An alternative available to these small organizations (and subunits of large organizations) is *synthetic validity* (Guion, 1965).

Synthetic validity basically involves the development of a test battery to predict specific components, elements, or aspects of jobs. For instance, suppose we wish to develop a selection system for several staff positions in ORG—the personnel manager and his staff, the marketing manager and his advertising and research and development staffs, and the finance manager and his accounting, legal, payroll, and operations staffs. The number of members in these subunits ranges from 1 to a maximum of ten. Careful job analyses identify the important elements of each of these functions. Figure 5.4 indicates the eight elements of the jobs included in the synthetic validity study in ORG.

The basic step in synthetic validity is to predict job elements. After we identify the elements in each job, we can proceed as we usually do in traditional validation. First, we develop criterion measures for these elements. Second, we examine potential predictors of these elements. The unique aspect of synthetic validity is the way we use data to test our hypothesized relationships. If we were interested in hiring someone for the operations staff, we would want to predict elements II, V, and IX. To predict element II we would use the data obtained from Managers, Personnel Staff, Advertising, Research and Development, Operations, and Legal. Thus, our data and subsequent relationship between potential predictor and the criterion measurement for element II are based on a sample size of 36 instead of 6 (Operations Staff). Prediction of the other elements is examined likewise; all of the jobs in which the element is important are combined. Decision making is the same in this procedure as in traditional validation with multiple criteria; the decision is based on the combined predictions for the elements of the job for which selection is being made.

		Managers	Personnel staff	Advertising	Research and development	Accounting	Payroll	Operations	Legal	Secretarial
I	Supervisory ability	✓				✓				
II	Decision making ability	✓	✓	✓	✓			✓	✓	
III	Reasoning ability	✓			✓				✓	
IV	Numerical ability		✓			✓	✓			
V	Skill in using computing machines		✓			✓	✓	✓		✓
VI	Creativity			✓	✓				✓	
VII	Public relations ability	✓	✓	✓					✓	✓
VIII	Speaking ability	✓							✓	✓
IX	Clerical skills		✓			✓	✓	✓		✓

FIGURE 5.4. *Composition of jobs to be included in synthetic validity study according to job components.*

The limitation to synthetic validity is that predictive and cross-validation are difficult because of the small number of people who apply for the jobs at one time or over a limited period of time. The basic advantages, though, are that a synthetic validity approach is more adaptable and flexible than traditional validation and does not require a large sample size. When jobs change, they change because their components change. We know through synthetic validity, however, which information sources predict the components; as the components change in a job, we need change only the corresponding predictor battery. This latter advantage indicates that the synthetic validity approach is appropriate for not only small but also large organizations.

Placement

Placement problems arise after a decision has been made to hire an applicant. The basis for this initial decision may have been that the applicant possesses "general" abilities that the company likes to see in its workers, or that he is number one in his class, or that he is returning to the organization after a leave of absence and his previous job has been filled. Regardless of the reason, the organization has a member without a specific position in mind.

The objectives of placement are to place each applicant in a position in which he will do his best work, or in a position so that each position is filled by someone who meets at least minimum requirements, or in a position so that the organization will receive maximum performance from the group of applicants as a whole. If we are trying to accomplish the first objective, we need to predict how well the applicant will do in each of the available positions. To accomplish this objective we could use regression analysis to obtain a predicted criterion score for each of the positions for which he is considered. The decision then would be to place the applicant on the job for which he has the highest predicted criterion value. Or, with *pattern analysis* we use the predictor information of those workers who are presently considered successful. Pattern analysis requires comparison of the applicant's predictor scores with the average predictor score values of successful workers in each position. Similarity between these scores is the basis for the placement decisions. The similarity is assessed by profile statistics, profile coefficients, or "distance from the standard" scores (Nunnally, 1967). A simple example of a decision based on similarity is illustrated in Figures 5.5 and 5.6. The average predictor score values for successful production workers are shown by the bold line in Figure 5.5; the values for successful salesmen are shown in Figure 5.6. The predictor scores of a single applicant have been superimposed as a dotted line on each figure. From the figures it is clear that the applicant is more like successful salesmen than successful workers.

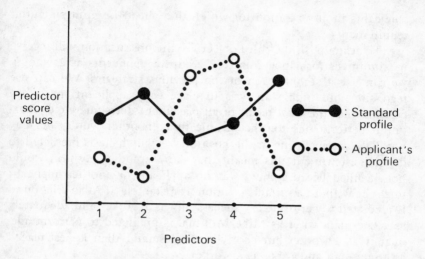

FIGURE 5.5. *Pattern of predictor scores for workers.*

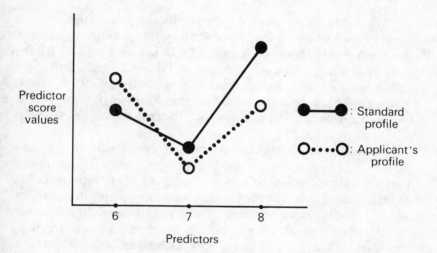

FIGURE 5.6. *Pattern of predictor scores for sales-men.*

If we are trying to accomplish the second objective (filling each position with an applicant who meets minimum requirements), we need to set a cutoff for the predictors of each position and place applicants in any position for which they meet the multiple cutoff requirements.

To accomplish the third objective (the organization will receive maximum performance from the group of applicants as a whole), we can use a combination of the previous strategies. We can use regression and profile analysis to place each applicant in such a position that the total result of all placement decisions yields maximum performance for the organization. In other words, we may not place an applicant in the position for which he is predicted to do his best work if this meant that either another position would not be filled because there was no applicant or another applicant might be without a suitable position. For example, if Allan Allaround is predicted to perform very successfully as a worker and adequately as a salesman, whereas Mike Minimal is predicted to perform adequately as a worker but poorly as a salesman, Allan is best placed as a salesman and Mike as a worker.

Prediction for Promotion and Transfer Decisions

We mentioned previously that predictor information sources could be used when we want to promote or transfer current workers. If we were considering a worker in ORG who has applied for the position of salesman, we might administer the same predictor battery to him as we would to an applicant from outside ORG. There is nothing different about the validation procedures whether the predictors are being used for promotion or transfer decisions or for initial selection.

Some organizations have established career ladders for their workers. If the interval of time between someone's entry into one position and promotion to the next is relatively brief, initial gathering of information may include predictors for the second step position. Again, there is nothing different about validation in this situation.

Another approach to promotions which is currently receiving considerable emphasis is the use of *assessment centers* (Bray & Grant, 1966). Those employees being considered for promotion receive extensive examination with a variety of techniques. This usually involves one to three days of testing, interviewing, and participating in simulated job activities. All workers at managerial levels often participate in assessment centers regardless of their level of interest in promotions. The information obtained is used to identify candidates with promotion potential and to provide feedback to the participants about their strengths and weaknesses. If information from assessment center examinations is used for promotion decisions it should be validated as in any other situation.

Unfair Discrimination and Selection Systems

Recent legislation (Civil Rights Act of 1964, Title VII), Supreme Court rulings (*Griggs vs. Duke Power*, March 1971) and guidelines (Equal Employment Opportunity Commission, 1970; Office of Federal Contract Compliance, 1971) have emphasized the problem of unfair discrimination towards minority groups and sexes with respect to selection and hiring. Unfair discrimination exists when applicants with equal probabilities of success on the job have unequal probabilities of being hired for the job (Guion, 1966).

One way to assess whether unfair discrimination exists is to divide the validity sample into groups on the basis of the variable of concern (race or sex) and compare the validity coefficients and the regression equations for each group. For example, Figure 5.7 illustrates the scatterplot for a case where two groups differ on average score on both the predictor and criterion, yet the regression equations are equal. In this case there is no unfair discrimination for there is equally good prediction for the two groups; the group that has the higher predictor scores (Group I) also is more successful on the criterion.

In contrast, the two groups in Figure 5.8 are equally successful on the criterion, but Group I scores higher on the predictor than Group II. Though the validity coefficients are equal, the regression equations are different. Consequently, if P_I is chosen as the cutoff, there would be unfair discrimination against Group II. One solution would be to have two cutoffs—P_I if the applicant is a member of Group I and P_{II} if the applicant is a member of Group II. Another solution would be to establish a separate regression equation for each group and to use the predicted criterion scores from the appropriate equation for each applicant. (An excellent article which illustrates interactions between predictor and criterion scores and their effect on heterogeneous or socially mixed groups is presented by Bartlett and O'Leary, 1969.)

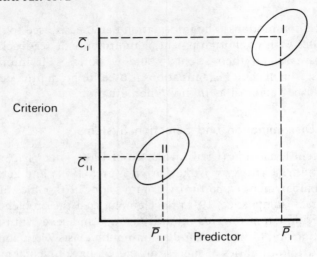

FIGURE 5.7. *Comparison of two groups (I and II) that differ on average score on the predictor (P) and criterion (C).*

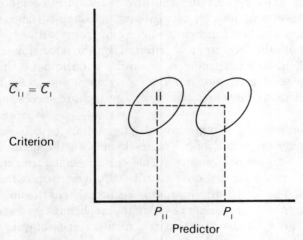

FIGURE 5.8. *Comparison of two groups that differ in performance on the predictor, but perform similarly on the criterion.*

With respect to whether discrimination exists, the burden of proof is on the employer. He must show that his predictor is related to performance and that the predictor is not differentially valid. To do this, the organization must conduct careful job analyses; develop reliable, relevant, and practical criterion measures; and perform appropriate and complete validity analyses.

Summary

In this chapter we have discussed the major concerns of the organization developing a selection program for obtaining members to fill its various positions. The major emphasis has been the strategies available for demonstrating a very basic theoretical statement—applicant *information sources* are related to *performance criteria*. We have examined, at considerable length, the traditional ways of validating performance criteria predictors. (Validation is nothing more than a test of the theoretical statement.) A review of the literature (Ghiselli, 1966) indicates that tests of this relationship in many organizations usually yield validity coefficients in the .30s and occasionally in the .40s and .50s. Though these coefficients do not have high absolute value, they have been demonstrated to have some utility, particularly if the selection ratio and base rate are taken into account.

Perhaps something other than the traditional linear validation models should be emphasized. Research on moderator variable approaches and types of pattern analyses may yield better frameworks within which to test the theoretical statement. Maybe we will be able to identify more appropriate information sources if we conduct careful, thorough job analyses. Job specific tests and job samples should receive more emphasis. Though personality tests have not been shown to be highly predictive of job performance (Guion & Gottier, 1965), this may be due to the points in time when both personality and criterion measurements are assessed. Typically, there is only a short interval between predictor measurements and criterion measurement. It is possible that personality variables are appropriate for longer term prediction or as moderators.

Finally, perhaps we should use trainability as a criterion, substituting training systems for some of our emphasis on selection systems. When obtaining members, an organization must be concerned not only with the selection process but how it may be coordinated with manpower planning programs, recruiting programs, and training programs, which we will discuss in the next chapter.

References

Job Choice

Crites, J. O. *Vocational psychology.* New York: McGraw, 1969.

Holland, J. L. *Psychology of vocational choice.* New York: Ginn, 1966.

Kuder, G. F. *Manual for the Kuder preference record—Vocational.* Chicago: Science Research Associates, 1960.

Roe, A. *Psychology of occupations.* New York: Wiley, 1956.

Strong, E. K., Jr. revised by D. P. Campbell. *Strong vocational interest blank: Manual.* Stanford, Calif.: Stanford University Press, 1966.

Super, D. E., & Bohn, M. J. *Occupational psychology.* Belmont, Calif.: Wadsworth, 1970.

Information Sources

Bray, D. W., & Grant, D. L. The assessment center in the measurement of potential for business management. *Psychological Monographs,* 1966, **80** (17, Whole No. 625).

Buros, O. K. (Ed.) *The seventh mental measurements yearbook.* Highland Park, N. J.: Gryphon, 1972.

Cronbach, L. J. *Essentials of psychological testing.* New York: Harper & Row, 1970.

Ghiselli, E. E. *The validity of occupational aptitude tests.* New York: Wiley, 1966.

Glennon, J. R., Albright, L. E., & Owens, W. A. *A catalog of life history items.* Reproduced by the Richardson Foundation, 1966.

Guion, R. M., & Gottier, R. F. Validity of personality measures in personnel selection. *Personnel Psychology,* 1965, **18,** 135–164.

Huck, J. R. Assessment centers: A review of the external and internal validities. *Personnel Psychology,* 1973, **26,** 191–212.

Mayfield, E. C. The selection interview—A re-evaluation of published research. *Personnel Psychology,* 1964, **17,** 239–260.

Meehl, P. E. *Clinical vs. statistical prediction.* Minneapolis: University of Minnesota Press, 1954.

Webster, E. C. *Decision making in the employment interview.* Montreal: Industrial Relations Centre, McGill University, 1964.

Wernimont, P. R., & Campbell, J. P. Signs, samples and criteria. *Journal of Applied Psychology,* 1968, **52,** 372–376.

Validation

American Psychological Association. *Standards for educational and psychological tests and manuals.* Washington: 1966.

Campbell, J. P. Cross-validation revisited. Paper presented at the meeting of the Midwestern Psychological Association, Chicago, 1967.

Chandler, R. E. Validity, reliability, baloney—and a little mustard. Paper presented at the meeting of the Midwestern Psychological Association, 1964.

Cronbach, L. J., & Gleser, G. C. *Psychological tests and personnel decisions.* Urbana, Ill.: University of Illinois Press, 1965.

Dunnette, M. D. *Personnel selection and placement.* Belmont, Calif.: Wadsworth, 1966.

Ghiselli, E. E. *Theory of psychological measurement.* New York: McGraw-Hill, 1964.

Gollob, H. F. Cross-validation in fixed effects analysis of variance. Paper presented at the meeting of the American Psychological Association, San Francisco, 1968.

Gollob, H. F. Cross-validation using samples of size one. Paper presented at the meeting of the American Psychological Association, Washington, D. C., 1967.

Guion, R. M. *Personnel testing.* New York: McGraw-Hill, 1965.

Mosier, C. I. Symposium: The need and means of cross-validation. I. Problems and designs of cross-validation. *Educational and Psychological Measurement,* 1951, **11,** 5–11.

Naylor, J. C., & Shine, L. C. A table for determining the increase in mean criterion score obtained by using a selection device. *Journal of Industrial Psychology,* 1965, **3,** 33–42.

Norman, W. T. Double-split cross-validation: An extension of Mosier's design, two undesirable alternatives, and some enigmatic results. *Journal of Applied Psychology,* 1965, **49,** 348–357.

Nunnally, J. C. *Psychometric theory.* New York: McGraw-Hill, 1967.

Taylor, H. C., & Russell, J. T. The relationship of validity coefficients to the practical effectiveness of tests in selection: Discussion and tables. *Journal of Applied Psychology,* 1939, **23,** 565–578.

Zedeck, S. Problems with the use of "moderator" variables. *Psychological Bulletin,* 1971, **76,** 295–310.

Unfair Discrimination

Bartlett, C. J., & O'Leary, B. S. A differential prediction model to moderate the effects of heterogeneous groups in personnel selection and classification. *Personnel Psychology,* 1969, **22,** 1–17.

Equal Employment Opportunity Commission. Guidelines on employee selection procedures. *Federal Register,* 1970, **35,** 12333 (1–3).

Guion, R. M. Employment tests and discriminatory hiring. *Industrial Relations,* 1966, **5,** 20–37.

Office of Federal Contract Compliance. Employee testing and other selection procedures. *Federal Register,* 1971, **36,** 19307–19310.

Personnel
Training and
Development

Everyone who enters an organization needs some training and does some learning. That is, every new member must gain some information about the organization and his role in it. Much of this information for new members is transmitted informally. Such matters as when and where the member will be paid, what dress standards are expected, which coworkers are most helpful, and so on are not usually part of a systematic training or orientation program, but must be learned by new members nonetheless. They are learned by observing others, by asking coworkers, and by noticing the personal consequences when behavioral boundaries are exceeded. In this chapter we will consider only formal training programs, but the reader should be aware of the amount of information picked up informally. It is reasonable to assume that most organizations depend on unsystematic teaching and learning for the transmission of some important information. Ambiguity and misinformation could be decreased, however, if these matters were included in formal training programs.

PURPOSES OF TRAINING

There are three purposes for a formal training program. The most familiar of these is the development of task knowledge or skills. Both new and incumbent employees sometimes participate in such courses. This is true at all levels of the organization—the executive studying linear programming as a decision-making tool, the engineer studying current developments in his specialty area, or the production employee practicing skills with technologically updated tools.

A second purpose for the formal training program is the transmission of information to orient the worker to the organizational or environmental context. Such training may include instructions about organizational policies. For example, new accountants may receive information about the accounting procedures in use throughout the organization, even though they will be involved in only a few of those procedures and it is assumed that they are already skilled in the necessary accounting techniques. Orientation training may be used to acquaint new workers with production or service goals or the structure (responsibility and authority) of the organization.

A third purpose for training is the modification of member attitudes. Often implicit in such training is the understanding that modification of attitudes will lead to modifications in task performance, but the training is not specifically designed to change task behavior. An example is the sensitivity training program (often called T-group or laboratory training) for managers. This type of training is sometimes an attempt to affect interpersonal attitudes with the expectation that interpersonal behavior will also change. Though managers' attitudes toward their subordinates may change or they may be more aware of how they are perceived by their subordinates, there may not be any change in the way they treat their subordinates. Another example of such training programs are those which attempt to change the work-related attitudes which hard-core unemployed bring to the work situation. Attempts also may be made to change the attitudes of incumbent workers who will be working alongside members of the disadvantaged group.

Training programs may be designed for more than one of these purposes. Opportunities Industrialization Centers (training programs for hard-core unemployed) attempt to teach skills and change work attitudes. Basic training in the Marine Corps involves job skills, information about the organization, and personal attitudes. Sales conferences may be for the purposes of transmitting organizational policy and changing attitudes (increasing optimism). Later in this chapter, we will discuss the importance of assessing the training program. It is impossible, however, to evaluate training unless its purposes have been carefully specified. Too often, even in formal educational programs, the purpose of a training program is defined so vaguely that no valid assessment is possible. If the purposes are specified in concrete terms, we can identify empirical indicators for theoretical units and form testable theoretical statements. "Workers trained on the job will produce more gadgets than workers trained in lecture sessions," for example, is a testable hypothesis.

PRELIMINARY QUESTIONS

Some basic questions should be answered before any training is begun. These questions are deceptively simple; their answers can be extremely difficult. The first and most crucial question is: "What are the training needs of the organization?" The answers to this question must specify who must be trained and what skills, information, or attitudes must be imparted. The second question is: "With what training techniques should the program be carried out?" And finally, "How will the training be evaluated?" No company would install an expensive new machine without ascertaining whether or not it was accomplishing the purpose for which it was purchased. The same perspective should be taken with the installation of any training program, which is almost sure to be expensive, if for no other reason than the man-hour investment. If the training need has been adequately specified (in answer to the first question above), it should be possible to determine whether the need has been met. Conversely, if it is not possible to measure whether the training program has accomplished its purpose, there is the probability that there was no clear purpose for the training.

Training departments, like most other subgroups of organizations, tend to become functionally autonomous. That is, they continue to exist and function even if their services are not required. One member of the ORG personnel staff may have primary responsibility for training and development. It is especially easy for the member in charge of training to justify his position in the organization without specifying his objective contribution. The attitude that "training is good" overshadows the necessity to demonstrate its contribution to the organization. If a member of the payroll staff institutes a new accounting procedure, it is usually justified on economical terms. However, if the training specialist institutes a new program, he is rarely asked to demonstrate its specific contribution. Such a policy is deficient; the training specialist should be required to show that his programs satisfy organizational needs.

Identifying Training Needs

ORGANIZATIONAL ANALYSIS

There are three approaches to questions about who should be trained and what the training content should be. The first is *organizational analysis*, an examination of the total organization. This requires that the investigator recognize the objectives, the resources (including manpower), and the environment (technological and socioeconomic) of the organization. The beginning point, as we have indicated is the case in most organizational research, is a careful statement of the long-term and short-term goals. These should be stated in terms which will allow an evaluation of the extent to which they are being met. The next point involves judgmental evaluations of the efficiency with which the organization's goals are being met. This is accomplished by criteria development and assessment. If efficiency or performance is judged to be poor, the training program is one alternative for improvement. Of course, depending on the inefficiencies, such alternatives as modification of goals, redefinition of the job, technological change, revision of selection practices, or change in the reward system may also be appropriate. Training is only one of several interdependent facets.

Underlying the need for training, one frequently finds situations categorized as *change*. The most obvious is a change in technology. This can occur at many places in the organization and can have widespread effects. Production methods may be altered in such a way that not only production workers but accounting and record-keeping personnel will have to adopt new techniques. If, for example, there is a change from individual production (for which piece-rates are the basis for compensation) to an assembly line, training is necessary for both production workers and other units in the organization. Foremen may have to be trained in new ways to evaluate performance. Accounting personnel may need to be trained to apply a new compensation scheme. Since salesmen may need to supply information in a new format, salesmen and sales managers also may need training. This situation creates a need for skill training, information transmission, and attitude modification and thus provides a setting for formal training programs.

Changes in *economic conditions* might also create a training need. As employment opportunities increase, those persons with the desired skills and information are hired first. If there are still jobs available, the unemployed and unskilled will require training. Training programs can develop skills, information, and attitudes among persons who would otherwise be unacceptable.

Characteristics of the work force also can change as a result of *social conditions.* An organization may draw its manpower from an area with a changing ethnic composition. For example, in one industrialized location the ethnic composition has changed in 20 years from predominantly Polish immigrant to predominantly black to predominantly Puerto Rican immigrant. Each ethnic group has its own set of work skills, information, and attitudes. Where these do not meet the organizational requirements, training is one way to accomplish a fit; of course, changes in the organization are also possible. Where such ethnic composition changes do take place, the supervisory personnel are often from the preceding ethnic group. Thus, in the example, Poles supervised blacks, and, later, blacks supervised Puerto Ricans. In such a case, a training program can acquaint supervisory personnel with the cultural backgrounds of the work force.

Training needs may be changed by more subtle and gradual changes in work force characteristics. For instance, over a period of years, personal backgrounds may change because of changes in school curricula, shifts in societal norms, rising educational levels of the general population, and so on.

Another factor which may lead to additions or changes in training programs is _societal demands_. From time to time changes occur in the obligations which society expects organizations to meet. A current example is the demand that industrial organizations provide job training for hard-core unemployed. Many organizations, in response, have undertaken such programs.

As an aside, let us discuss some aspects of training programs for hard-core unemployed. Initially, it was believed that the training of hard-core unemployed involved primarily job skills and job information. But investigation demonstrated that trainee job attitudes and life style were at least as important as skills and information. The hard-core unemployed not only lack the ability to do skilled work, they often have had so little contact with work in an industrial society that they do not have the living habits or expectations necessary to cope with a regular job. For example, they may not be used to getting up at a regular time five days a week to go to work. Training programs have used a variety of techniques to adapt trainees' work habits, work attitudes, and work expectations: (1) the inclusion of rewards (financial compensation) during the training program as encouragement to complete training; (2) the guarantee of employment at the end of the training program; (3) the removal of trainees from their habitual environment in an effort to change habits, attitudes, or associations that diminish the effectiveness of training; and (4) the assignment to each trainee of a "buddy" who has considerable work experience and can serve as a behavior model for the trainee, helping him in his personal adjustment to the new situation.

It is difficult to assess the success of training programs for hard-core unemployed since performance standards sometimes are modified explicitly and implicitly. Staying on the job is sometimes the only measured criterion. Attempts to measure changes in work attitudes or expectations are rare. Theoretical statements can be formulated and tested, however, to examine the relationships between the *techniques* listed above and the *criteria*. For example, *"Type of compensation* (during or at the end of training) is related to *work attitudes."* This section does not apply exclusively to the hard-core unemployed; such techniques and concerns are appropriate for all trainee groups.

JOB ANALYSIS

Training needs also can be identified through *job analysis*. Procedures for job analyses were discussed in Chapter Three. Those who need training can be identified by evaluation of the performance of current workers (see Chapter Four) and comparison with the job demands specified in job analyses. Program content can be organized around the information contained in the job analysis. This approach assumes that the job analysis is accurate; analyses should be checked periodically to insure that they keep pace with the inevitable changes in organizations and jobs.

Job analyses which have been constructed from *behavioral expectation* information (see Chapter Four) can be quite useful in developing training programs. This format provides a description of the job in terms of required work behaviors. The training program can be developed to teach the expected behaviors and the situations in which they are required rather than generalities. Specific examples of good and bad job performance are available for trainees to see, and if the behavioral expectations items are used in performance evaluation scales, workers can be trained and evaluated on the same dimensions.

MANPOWER ANALYSIS

A third perspective for identifying training needs is *manpower analysis*, which focuses on the individual worker rather than the job. The cultural background, educational level, work history, performance evaluations, and work sample and knowledge tests of the individual workers should be considered. With this information judgments can be made about the need for training on the present job or the possibility of training the worker for other jobs.

If an organization's personnel policies are thoughtfully planned, they will include information about present and projected growth and turnover rates in the various jobs. Given the possibility of predicting future worker needs, training programs can enable present employees to qualify for higher positions and progress through career ladders. For example, a career ladder could be developed in the finance subunit of ORG. Persons hired as business machine operators on the payroll staff could be trained for accounting tasks; persons in accounting might be trained for future positions as accounting supervisors or other managerial positions. Such a program has obvious advantages for both workers and the organization: workers are able to develop new skills and progress in their careers; organizations can hire for lower positions and develop staff for higher positions rather than hiring initially at the higher level where the costs of recruiting and selection are greater.

Relation of Training to Selection

Our discussion has implied a relationship between training and selection which now will be made more explicit. The relationship is simple and direct. It is possible to avoid formal training programs by selecting people who already have the necessary or desired skills. Conversely, it is possible to select untrained persons by providing training. Both selection and training have costs for the organization. If the organization can afford to be very selective, it can forego some training; if it can afford a great deal of training, it can be less selective. Job applicants who already possess the necessary skills usually cost more in recruitment and pay. If these costs are excessive, or if trained applicants are not available, the proper solution may be to train the untrained applicants.

The decision, of course, depends on the specific situation and will often combine selection and training. For example, no industry is likely to train engineers. Even though it is more expensive to hire engineers than high school graduates, the costs of an engineering education to the organization are too great to compensate for any savings in selection. Some industries, however, do have summer training programs or internship semesters so that students will get training in the specific problems of the industry.

If persons in lower organizational levels are trained for, and move to, higher levels, of course, selection procedures should be focused on supplying new persons at the lower levels and should include a prediction of applicant trainability. The reader will recognize by now that training and selection are interrelated and related to decisions about job definition, organizational structure, and performance evaluation.

Basic Principles Involved in Training

The underlying goal in the development and operation of training techniques is the facilitation of learning; the principles related to this goal are adopted by trainers to improve the effectiveness of the training program. Each of these principles could be developed into a theoretical statement and should be tested empirically.

MOTIVATION

If any training program is to be successful, the participants must want to learn; they should approach training with a positive attitude. The training program should be intrinsically and extrinsically rewarding. *Intrinsic motivation* is affected by the interest, meaningfulness, and perceived personal utility of the material to be learned. *Extrinsic motivation* is a result of the value the organization places on training—that is, benefits and promotions or other rewards provided by the organization—and will affect attendance in the training program. Motivation will be influenced by whether attendance is voluntary, forced, or "suggested"; learning will be affected by the kind and degree of pressure exerted by the organization.

A basic problem is the optimal degree of motivation necessary for success in the training program. Because "not enough" or "too much" motivation may lead to poor performance on many tasks and situations, the trainer should investigate the degree to which participants need to be motivated and the degree to which motivation must vary, if at all, in the training period.

Another problem is the possibility of different levels or types of motivation depending on whether participants are current or potential workers. If potential workers believe that the success of their application depends on their performance in the training program, their motivation may be much greater than that of current workers who may be participating to maintain skills or gain information to facilitate promotion. If both groups are in the same program, different rewards may be necessary.

KNOWLEDGE OF RESULTS

One way to motivate is to provide knowledge of results, or feedback, to the trainee. Immediate feedback makes the training task more interesting and allows the trainee to correct his performance. The factor inhibits the learning of incorrect behaviors which can occur if feedback is withheld until completion of the training program. It should be pointed out that the type of feedback is important—informing the trainee that he is wrong is not as valuable as telling him what is wrong *and* explaining how his performance can be improved.

PARTICIPATION AND PRACTICE

For maximum effectiveness, learned behavior must be practiced and repeated and should involve active participation during the course of training. The problem is to determine the necessary amount of practice or overlearning.

MASSED OR DISTRIBUTED LEARNING

Should the learning, participation, and practice be undertaken in a short, concentrated period (massed) or should training be drawn out (distributed) over a long period? Such factors as the time available to the trainer and trainees, the cost of the trainer, and the cost to the trainees and organization will influence how the content is taught. Theoretical statements pertaining to the degree to which learning is massed or distributed should be formulated and tested to determine the optimal strategy.

WHOLE OR PART LEARNING

Related to massed and distributed practice is the problem of whole or part learning. In other words, how much of the content should be presented at a given time? Can the content be divided into segments or is it best presented as a whole before emphasizing parts?

TRANSFER OF TRAINING

These five principles are not independent; their implementation should facilitate transfer of training, or application of the training content to the work setting. After all, the results of training should be reflected on the job. When we discuss the evaluation of training programs later in this chapter, the degree of transfer of training will be the focus.

The basic principles of training, which involve how content is learned, are not, however, the sole considerations when designing a program. Another important consideration is the _task to be learned_ (Gagné, 1962). The task components, the content to be learned, and the sequence of learning must be identified. Essentially, we are concerned with job and task analyses and with what is to be learned and how.

The final consideration is _individual differences._ The type of individual involved in training—his interest, ability, aptitude, and personality—will interact with the task to be learned, the learning process (principles), and the trainer's characteristics. The implication is that, ideally, we should consider different teaching methods for different types of trainees.

Methods for Training and Development

The choice of training or development procedure depends on the factors discussed above. The theoretical orientation of the training specialist and the degree to which he incorporates various training principles, the type of job or task for which one is to be trained, the types of individuals who will participate in the program, and the level in the organization for which the training is designed will influence procedure. Another factor is the time at which training is to be given. The training might be: (1) prior to employment (when success in training assures a position); (2) during the initial stages of employment prior to placement; (3) at specified times in the work experience; (4) prior to advancement or promotion; or (5) at the convenience of the organization and the participants. Finally, and perhaps most important, is the purpose of training. Will factual, specific skills, content, and general information or general development in decision making, communications, and human relations be emphasized?

Training Methods for Specific Abilities and Information

Regardless of the content to be learned, most new or promoted workers receive some _orientation_ with respect to the type of job, the job environment and conditions, and the organizational roles, policies, and objectives. This sort of information should be presented clearly and concisely in a short time. The easiest teaching method is the _lecture_ (classroom experience) or a _conference._ The lecture allows one trainer to present new information to a large group in a relatively short time. The company can televise, film, or videotape the initial session and repeat it at its convenience. The disadvantages are obvious; there is little, if any, participation or feedback to the trainees and the necessity of having an outstanding lecturer to stimulate and motivate the participants.

The conference provides new information and allows active participation in a small group. As a result of the conference, each employee should understand the organization's goals and policies and have an opportunity to raise questions and challenge certain areas.

Most training methods are designed to teach new facts and concepts, provide specific information, and develop skills. *On-the-job* training permits the trainee to learn while performing in the actual setting under supervision. The advantages to the trainee are obvious: active participation; feedback; reality (as opposed to simulation); and no problem of transfer of training. For the organization there is no need for special equipment or space, no need for training specialists (incumbent workers are the trainers), and the trainee contributes to productivity while learning. There are some costs to the organization, however, since learning is slower in on-the-job than off-the-job training procedures.

Specific on-the-job methods are *coaching, apprenticeship,* and *job rotation.* Coaching requires a one-to-one relationship between the supervisor (who may be a worker or official supervisor) and the trainee. It is an effective procedure only if the relationship between the two is perceived as beneficial to both. The coach must be accomplished in the task and must serve as a role model, but he also must avoid having the trainee become dependent upon him.

Apprenticeship also involves a one-to-one learning experience but often in conjunction with classroom instruction. The trainee serves as an apprentice for a fixed and usually extended period of time before he becomes a journeyman. The fixed length of the program is a weakness because it ignores individual learning differences.

Job rotation moves the trainee from one position to another over a period of time and permits him to observe and participate in various functions and tasks. Usually the movement is to successively advanced positions; job rotation is most often used to prepare trainees for managerial positions. The trainee benefits from contact with various supervisors, learns the interrelationship among departments and tasks, and, at the same time, contributes to the various departments. If a salesman in ORG is being prepared for the position of sales manager, he may spend some time in the personnel office, the advertising department, research and development, and accounting in order to learn how those functions influence and are influenced by sales.

Off-the-job training procedures can be as specific as on-the-job, if there is adequate simulation, and allow the presentation of supplemental information. Off-the-job training also allows for trial-and-error learning whereas on-the-job training must emphasize both learning *and* production. Other advantages are that the organization can be flexible in the type of instruction and how and when it is offered. The major problems pertain to transfer of training and trainee motivation and reinforcement. It is often difficult for a trainee to realize the value of instruction in any but the actual situation.

Vestibule training is one form of off-the-job training in which training specialists operate in a simulated work environment with similar equipment and materials. The concern is solely with learning, and the transfer of training problem is diminished. The trainee also has the advantages of active participation, feedback, and time for practice. The obvious disadvantages are the costs of simulation, duplicating equipment, and using materials.

Business games are a form of simulation used to instruct in the economics of the organization and, as previously mentioned, in decision-making principles. Rules, derived from economic theories, specify the relationships between inputs (raw materials, capital, equipment, and personnel) and outputs (quantity sold and profit) as influenced by such factors as wages and salaries, budget, company policy, and economic conditions. The trainee, on the basis of certain inputs, decides what action the organization should take, for example, in price setting, hiring rates, advertising, research, and investments. Depending on the complexity of the games (many use computers), feedback is received rapidly and reflects such consequences of the decisions as profits and losses, surveys, marketing analyses, and extensive financial reports. One point of the games is to demonstrate the interrelationships between various parts and functions of the organization and how decisions affect all parts.

Business games involve the participants, provide feedback, encourage trial and error, and are usually motivating. The disadvantage is that results and feedback are based on how the game is programmed. A valid but novel approach may not be recognized. Also, the trainee may respond differently to the rewards of the game and real-life situations.

The *case study* is similar to business games. Various aspects of an organizational operation are described on paper, and the trainee is required to identify problems and offer solutions. A small group usually analyzes and discusses the same case; consequently, the participant receives feedback from others. The in-basket technique (described in Chapter Two) combines some features of the case study and business games.

Finally, *programmed instruction* involves a detailed analysis of the program content—breaking it down into small elements—and requires active participation at the individual's own pacing and provides feedback. One general procedure requires the trainee to read a brief paragraph and then respond in writing to a question. The correct response is immediately compared to the trainee's response; if it matches, the trainee moves on to another paragraph and the procedure is repeated. If the trainee's response is incorrect, he is directed to another place in the text where the concept is discussed again. The advantage is that all learning principles are supposedly incorporated, but the disadvantage is the degree of transfer of training which occurs.

Training Methods for General Organizational Development

Organizational development (OD) is a planned learning process whereby the organization members increase total organizational effectiveness as a result of increased interpersonal awareness in the work environment. The purposes of OD are to improve trust among employees and groups throughout the organization, increase knowledge about individual and group processes and dynamics, increase the sense of belonging to and being part of the organization, and create an open environment in which all individuals can work together for the common goals. Three procedures are used to achieve these purposes: *role playing; sensitivity training;* and *empirical feedback*.

Role playing involves the assumption of a position not actually occupied by the role player. As an example, the worker "acts out" a problem situation in which he assumes the role of foreman. This technique enables the employee to examine a problem from a different perspective, gain experience in problem-solving, and increase his self-awareness and insights into others. The success of role playing depends on how well the participants assume and act out the roles. If successful, role playing allows participants to try out various solutions to human relations problems and to receive feedback from others about their behavior and problem-solving methods. But role playing is time consuming, and the newly-learned human relations skills may be difficult to transfer to everyday situations.

Sensitivity training (T-groups, encounter groups) is a small-group situation in which the behaviors exhibited in the group are explored and analyzed. The group has no task other than providing discussion and feedback of such observed interpersonal behaviors as communications ability, defense mechanisms, and emergent leadership. When the participant returns to his organization he is expected to be more aware of his behavior and how he is perceived.

Sensitivity training formats vary as to length of meeting, role of the trainer, size of the group, and type of supplements used (for example, lectures and group exercises). Regardless of the format, one assumption is that participants can provide articulate and constructive feedback in a psychologically safe yet anxiety-provoking situation. The facts that the temporary meeting is in an isolated environment, that the heterogeneous group does not know each other at the beginning and probably will not meet again, and that the meeting is nonevaluative all discourage chances for transfer of training.

The *managerial grid* is one way of using sensitivity training in OD (Blake & Mouton, 1964). This approach is concerned primarily with how participants are perceived and the development of managerial skills. The goal is to teach a management style which includes concern for both people and production. The approach assumes that successful managers can achieve the organizational goals by involving their subordinates in organizational processes. A form of T-group is used to learn how a manager is perceived, exercises and case problems are used to illustrate managerial style, and that behavior is the focus of another T-group session.

Empirical feedback techniques make intraorganizational measurements of workers' attitudes and perceptions of the organization and supervision. Information from this organization-wide survey is then summarized and returned to the members for discussion. Supervisors have an opportunity to see how they are perceived by their subordinates, and subordinates have an opportunity to compare their own perceptions of the organization with those of their coworkers. This procedure is usually carried out periodically with the aid of personnel, specifically trained to facilitate organizational change and development, who are referred to as change agents. These periodic assessments indicate whether the specified changes (usually improvements in communications, decision making, and member participation) are taking place.

Evaluation

We have discussed *how* content can be taught in organizations and have referred to the general areas of *what* is taught. Campbell, Dunnette, Lawler, and Weick (1970) have labeled as *modifiers* the set of characteristics that influences training and interacts with the "how" and "what." Whether the training is on company or employee time, total training time, training locale (inside or outside the company), who does the training (line, staff, or external training specialist), and the motivation of trainer and trainee influence training results. Modifiers interact with the content, the method, and the participants. The implication is that the company and the individual have more than one combination to use to accomplish the training goals.

Once the training program is developed, it is as necessary to validate it as it is necessary to validate a selection system. Did the training program accomplish the intended goals? Did the training program justify the time and cost? How is one training program better than others? How much training should be given? When are plateaus (no increase in learning for a period of time) reached? What are the effects of overlearning? The basic question is, however: What are the criteria for evaluation of training programs?

Criteria

We have indicated that the general purposes of training are to teach skills, provide factual information, or affect human relations. These purposes dictate the criteria. *Opinion* is a simple criterion for the success or failure of the program. Most individuals indicate their feelings about the value of the program but, because they have been involved, the weight of their opinions should be minimized. It is unwise to pay too much attention to either the company representative who bought the training program or to the planner of the program who, at the conclusion of training, announces that the program was a success. (However, if the representative concludes that the program was a failure, this should be treated the same as negative information in a reference letter.) Likewise, it is unwise to weigh too highly the opinion of the trainer or even the participants, who may know the purpose of the training and intentionally or unintentionally, bias their evaluation.

There are more direct, objective, and better criteria. *Attitude change* indicates whether participants have different attitudes and if these correspond to the purposes of training. *Objective examinations* or *work samples* can be used to determine if the participants have learned a task or factual information. These particular measures may be taken at the conclusion of the training program. When and how often to measure, however, depends on whether the training program goals were short or long term.

When the training goals are long term and are to affect the entire organization, it may be best to use different criteria for different levels in the organization. Suppose product supervisors participate in an OD program. We might assess the program by measuring the amount of attitude and behavior change after participation. For foremen and workers, however, we might assess the effects by measuring performance, productivity, and attitudes.

Evaluation Research Designs

An evaluation research design should facilitate unambiguous understanding of training program effects. Designs vary with respect to the number of groups receiving training, the number of control groups, whether there is a determination of performance or attitude prior to training, and when and how many criterion measurements are made (see Figure 6.1).

The simplest way to assess training is to obtain criterion measurements on the group of trainees *after* training (see Figure 6.1a). This is fast and inexpensive but of little value since only an "after" measure (C) is taken and there is no assessment of change. Though we can know the absolute performance level after training, we don't know if that performance level is better, poorer, or the same as performance prior to training. The *before-after* assessment of the training group (see Figure 6.1b) assesses the change in the criterion for the trainees but does not allow us to state with much confidence that the change was due to training. It is possible that other events were occurring in the organization, that employees were naturally improving in performance, or that a Hawthorne effect was operating.

To alleviate the ambiguities inherent in the *after* and *before-after* designs we can employ one or more *control group designs.* If we obtain before-after measures on both the training group and a control group (see Figure 6.1c), we assume all organizational factors (except the Hawthorne effect) are affecting the two groups similarly and any differences on training criteria are due to some aspect of training.

Training
group C_1 T C_2

Control
$T \cdot C$ C_1 T C_2 group C_1 C_2

(a)   (b)   (c)

Training group C_1 T C_2 Training group C_1 T C_2
Control group C_1 C_2 Control group C_1 C_2
Control group C_1 P C_2 Control group $\bar{X}_{C_1}$ T C_2

(d)   (e)

Training group C_1 T C_2
Control group C_1 P C_2
Control group C_1 C_2
Control group C_2

(f)

FIGURE 6.1. *Evaluation research designs* (C = *criterion measurement;* T = *training;* P = *placebo).*

To reduce the possibility that change is due to the Hawthorne effect and not primarily to training, we can employ before and after measures on the training group and *two control groups* (see Figure 6.1d). The additional control group can serve two purposes. First, it can be given a treatment that serves as a placebo (P) that arouses the Hawthorne effect but does not produce any relevant learning. For example, the performance level of one work group would be assessed on the criterion (C_1), the group would be trained (T) in ways of improving performance, and it would be reassessed (C_2) on the criterion after training. A second group would provide only the two criterion measurements (C_1 and C_2); it would receive no training. The third group would be assessed on the performance criterion (C_1), would receive instruction about a potential new health plan (P), and would be reassessed on the criterion (C_2). If the improvement in performance is the same for the first and third groups, we can conclude that improvement is due to the increased attention of the training situation and not the training itself. If the training is effective, the differences between the before and after performance assessments should be greater for the training group than for either the placebo or regular control group.

The second use of the two-control group is to control for the interaction effects of before measures on training (see Figure 6.1e), especially when the criterion is an attitude measure. Any time we ask questions or test there is the possibility that we affect behavior. Consequently, the design would call for administering before and after measures to the training group and *one* control group. The second control group would not receive the before measures but, in analysis, would assume the average of the before measures for the first control group and the training group ($\overline{X}_{C_1}$). A difference between the *assumed* before and the *actual* after measures (C_2) should indicate, then, that training is effective. If there is no difference between the training group and the second control group, on the other hand, there is no interaction between the before measures and the training.

A *three-control group* (Solomon, 1949) also checks on the interaction effects of pretesting and training (see Figure 6.1f). One control group receives before and after measurement and a placebo. The second control group receives before and after measurement and no training or placebo. The third control group receives only an after measure and no training or placebo. The effects of the before measure are indicated by a comparison of the second and third control groups.

These control group designs are good from a research point of view. Organizations desiring to develop a training program often will not be large enough, however, to form control and training groups of the size necessary for analysis. It is also unlikely that management will be able to justify giving training to one group and not others. The solution may be the use of one of two quasi-experimental designs (Campbell & Stanley, 1963) which are not ideal but tend to test the effects of training versus nontrivial alternative explanations.

The *time series analysis* requires measurement of the criterion on several occasions both prior to and after training, all measurements on the training group. If training is effective, the slope, or intercept, of the curve relating performance to time should change after training. Figure 6.2 shows two situations: line A illustrates effective training and line B illustrates a situation in which one cannot conclude that training is effective without additional investigation. The relative increase in performance in situation B was obvious before training and was maintained after training. If we had taken only one before and one after measure in situation B, we would have incorrectly concluded that training was effective. In contrast, A shows a change as a result of training that is maintained over a period of time.

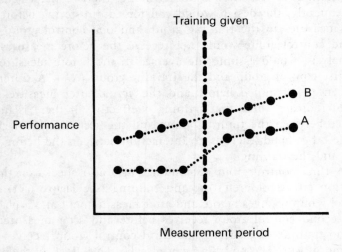

FIGURE 6.2. *Time series analysis.*

A second quasi-experimental design is *institutional cycle analysis* (see Figure 6.3), useful in situations for which control groups are impossible. Suppose we wish to institute a training program for keypunch operators. A class of trainees would be measured on their keypunching ability prior to training (at time 1) and their skills would be reassessed after training (time 2). At this time another class would be assessed prior to training. The second class is also assessed at the completion of training (time 3). (At this time another class might begin and the sequence would be continued.) At time 2, therefore, the second class begins to serve as a control group for the first training class. The before and after measures of the first class are compared with the before measures of the second class. Comparison of C_2 of the first training group with C_1 of the second training group indicates the effectiveness of training. Comparison of C_1 of the first training group with C_1 of the second training group is also necessary to show that a difference in the first comparison is not due to the first group's initially higher performance level.

	TIME 1	TIME 2	TIME 3	TIME 4
FIRST TRAINING GROUP	$C_1 T$	C_2		
SECOND TRAINING GROUP		$C_1 T$	C_2	
THIRD TRAINING GROUP			$C_1 T$	C_2

FIGURE 6.3. *Institutional cycle analysis* (C = *criterion measurement;* T = *training*).

Summary

In this chapter we have discussed the purposes of training, the development of training programs, ways for determining where training is needed in the organization, the content of training programs, and specific methods for conducting and evaluating training programs. We have also indicated that decisions concerning training programs are related to selection systems, job design, career ladders, and so on.

The essential point, however, is that training programs must be evaluated. Evaluation of training is as necessary as validation of a selection procedure. The utility and practical aspect of improvement as well as the statistical significance of changes due to training should be considered. Multiple criteria should be used and their interrelationships examined. Performance and attitudinal criteria should be assessed and their relationships to each other and training should be studied. If training is successful and leads to adequately rewarded performance and worker satisfaction, the organization will maintain itself.

References

General Training and Development

Bass, B. M., & Vaughan, J. A. *Training in industry: The management of learning.* Belmont, Calif.: Wadsworth, 1966.

Blake, R. R., & Mouton, J. S. *The managerial grid.* Houston: Gulf, 1964.

Campbell, J. P. Personnel training and development. *Annual Review of Psychology,* 1971, **22,** 565–602.

Campbell, J. P., & Dunnette, M. D. Effectiveness of T-group experiences in managerial training and development. *Psychological Bulletin,* 1968, **70,** 73–104.

Campbell, J. P., Dunnette, M. D., Lawler, E. E., & Weick, K. E. *Managerial behavior, performance, and effectiveness.* New York: McGraw-Hill, 1970.

Gagné, R. M. Military training and principles of learning. *American Psychologist,* 1962, **17,** 83–91.

Mager, R. F., & Pipe, P. *Analyzing performance problems or "you really oughta wanna."* Belmont, Calif.: Fearon, 1970.

McGehee, W., & Thayer, P. W. *Training in business and industry.* New York: Wiley, 1961.

Research Design

Campbell, D. T., & Stanley, J. C. *Experimental and quasi-experimental designs for research.* Chicago: Rand McNally, 1963.

MacKinney, A. C. Progressive levels in the evaluation of training programs. *Personnel,* 1957, **34,** 72–77.

Sellitz, C., Jahoda, M., Deutsch, M., & Cook, S. W. *Research methods in social relations.* New York: Holt, Rinehart, & Winston, 1962.

Solomon, R. L. An extension of control group design. *Psychological Bulletin,* 1949, **46,** 137–150.

Maintaining the Organization

Reward Systems

We are now at the stage of trying to maintain the organization as an on-going, efficient, and effective entity. In Section I we described the problems and considerations of establishing organizations; in Section II we discussed the problems and considerations of obtaining and developing organization members. Here we are concerned with the maintenance of the organization—that is, maintaining an environment that is conducive to effective and efficient worker functioning and encourages the worker to remain in the organization.

Reward systems play a major role in a worker's decision to join and remain a member of the organization; they have been used to attempt to satisfy and motivate employees. Briefly defined, reward systems are those job-related factors (derived from the organization, work groups, the job, or within the individual) that affect an individual's relationship to the organization and his job role. Examples of reward systems are salary and wage policies, incentives (financial and nonfinancial), and work values and goals.

This chapter focuses on pay and its relationship to organizational effectiveness. There are several reasons for devoting an entire chapter to pay. First, it is the one reward used by all except volunteer organizations. Second, a considerable amount of research has been devoted to the effects of pay on work attitudes and job performance (see Lawler, 1971). Perhaps this is because pay is the most tangible of rewards—easy to speak of, control, change, and observe. Third, pay satisfaction has been used as both an independent and dependent variable in theoretical statements. That is, research has examined both the *effects* of low and high pay satisfaction and the *causes* of various levels of pay satisfaction. Here we will discuss pay with respect to wage and salary administration and to how it is perceived.

Job Evaluation

A *job evaluation* is one use of the job analysis (see Chapter Three) which has identified the elements of job performance. The job evaluation establishes a monetary reward scheme that reflects the relative worth of the elements of performance, the nature of the work, and the effort expended. It is a systematic attempt, employing subjective appraisals of the job and its worth to the organization, to establish equitable (and minimum and maximum) pay rates for jobs.

There are two basic steps in all job evaluation procedures. First, all jobs must be analyzed, evaluated, and scaled along a continuum of worth or value to the organization. Second, the scales of worth must be translated into monetary values. These two steps are usually accomplished by *job evaluation committees* composed of company representatives, union or labor representatives, and possibly a "neutral" job evaluation specialist. The heterogeneity of the committee facilitates the establishment of a fair monetary reward scheme, and acceptance by labor and management is more likely to occur if both are represented.

Step I. Evaluating the Worth of the Job to the Organization

The *ranking method*, one of several evaluation procedures, requires the committee members to rank order the jobs with respect to importance. It is a simple and expedient process with, however, severe drawbacks. Ranking requires consideration of the overall value of each job. There is little, if any, consideration of the *specific* aspects or components of each job and this diminishes the ability to compare jobs or to use present jobs as standards for future jobs. Overall judgments may necessitate comparing scarcity of applicants for one job with the essential nature of the work on another job with job hazards of a third. Specific differences between jobs are not readily apparent. It is relatively easy to distinguish between the most important and least important jobs. If we consider only overall worth to the organization, however, it may be more difficult to distinguish between research and development, advertising, and other positions in the middle of the job continuum. Finally, as pointed out in the discussion of performance appraisals (Chapter Four), ranking is suitable when only a small number of subjects are to be ranked.

The *classification method* is a similar procedure in which the committee establishes and describes *broad* labor grades or job classifications. Specific jobs are fitted within this general schedule. An example is the Federal Civil Service General Schedule in which all civil service jobs (ranging from clerical to heads of bureaus) are classified into one of 18 job grades. Jobs that are perceived as being of equal worth are placed in the same grade.

This procedure, like the ranking method, considers jobs with respect to overall value to the company and has similar disadvantages. The advantage to this method, however, is that it reduces the number of jobs considered simultaneously. That is, if we had 30 jobs, *ranking* requires a delineation between each of the 30; *classification* requires that each of the 30 jobs be placed in, for example, one of six grades.

The *factor comparison method* is one procedure which considers the components of each job. It requires the committee to examine and identify the factors or elements in all jobs. (This information may be available from job descriptions or the results of a synthetic validity project.) Suppose the committee determines that five factors are required for the various jobs in the organization: mental ability; manual skill; physical ability; responsibility; and suitable working conditions. Once the factors are defined, a small group of existing key jobs is identified which reflects the range and salary rates agreed upon as equitable in the organization, community, and industry.

The key jobs are ranked twice. First, each job is ranked with respect to each factor. For example, if there are 12 key jobs, they are ranked from lowest to highest with respect to the mental ability factor, then the manual skill factor, and so on. Second, each job is assessed with respect to how much of the present hourly wage is appropriate to each factor. That is, if the present hourly rate for the job of worker is four dollars, one possible apportionment would be:

	Mental Ability	Manual Skill	Physical Ability	Responsibility	Working Conditions
Worker	$.80	$2.00	$.85	$.20	$.15

Similar apportionments are made for other key jobs and the jobs are compared for rank position on each of the factors.

In essence, then, each job has a ranking based on wage apportionment and another based on factor composition. The two rankings should be similar. If the job of worker is paid at four dollars per hour and the job of maintenance man is paid at three dollars per hour and both require mental ability but the job of worker requires more, the dollar wage apportionment for mental ability should be greater for the job of worker than for maintenance man. If there are discrepancies between the two rankings for one job, they should either be resolved or the job should be dropped from the "key" list. The final list of key jobs is used as a standard. Each new job is evaluated and ranked according to its major elements. Determination of job salary level would depend on how the job fits into the wage apportionments of the key job list.

The major problem with this procedure is the selection of "key" jobs and factors. The basis for selection is usually overall job value to the organization, and, as already indicated, defining overall value can be a problem. Also, because selection and assessment depends on current workers, their ways of work, and their present salary schedules, the final evaluation may reflect current inequities among the key jobs.

A final procedure is the *points method*, which also requires the identification of factors in all jobs. Once the factors are identified, levels within each factor are delineated and points are assigned to each level. The sums of points for the levels can be equal or vary from factor to factor. Suppose we identify the same five factors used in our discussion of the factor comparison method. With the points method we denote various levels for each of the factors—for example, we might have five levels of manual skill. The evaluation committee might assign points ranging from 15–80 to each of the levels. There might also be five levels for the responsibility factor, but the points might have another range, say 5–40. (The lower number of points might be because responsibility is not as important a factor in the set of jobs being considered.) Each job is then evaluated with respect to each factor and its levels and the corresponding points. The result is a summation of points on the five factors for each job and a consequent differentiation between jobs.

In summary, job evaluation is primarily a determination of the worth of the job to the organization. The criterion in all cases being a *subjective judgment of worth*, the main problem is to define *worth* and measure it reliably.

Step II. Converting Job Evaluation Results to Monetary Units

The above-mentioned procedures are straightforward, administrative acts. The major concern, however, is the impact on the worker when the points or units are converted to salary schedules. We are particularly interested in the *perception* of the wage rates and the influence of that perception on performance. Conversion requires establishing a correspondence between salary levels and the continuum of points (or factors, levels, or rank order); that is, it requires the plotting of points against salary levels.

Whether the shape of the salary schedule curve is a linear or power function is important (see Figure 7.1). The height of the curve at any particular point indicates the value and prestige of the job

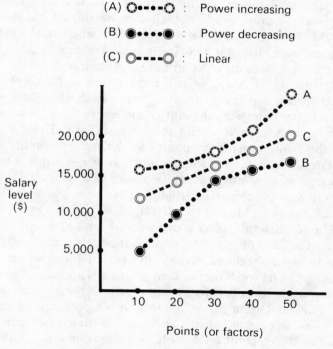

FIGURE 7.1. *Salary schedule curves.*

at that point. The shape of the curve suggests the rate of salary advancement and reflects the organization's perception of the difference between jobs. In the figure, curve A (increasing power function) might represent a particular job family. As we go up the ladder in the job family there is a greater and greater increment. The organization places more value on high-level jobs since the difference between two jobs at the high end reflects a greater increase in salary than the difference between two low-level jobs. In contrast, the jobs at the high end of curve B (power decreasing function) reflect less reward difference than the jobs at the low end. On curve C (linear function), equal distances on the point dimension result in equal differences in the salary structure.

Another concern in establishing the curves (as in Figure 7.1) is the *reference curve*. Should the curve be developed specifically for the plant (or office) or should it reflect or be comparable to the organizational or even industry curve? Answers will depend on economic and social conditions, geographic factors, community variables, labor-management relations, and so on. The reference curve is important because it affects both the selection of members and maintenance of the organization. An organization might establish a different wage curve for an office in mid-Manhattan than it would for the same jobs in an office in Princeton, Indiana.

Related to the shape of the curve is the *width of the wage bracket* for given points or factors. It is unlikely that there will be one salary level for each job point group; rather there are minimum and maximum salary levels for the job point level. Figure 7.2 illustrates the minimum and maximum wage rates for a family of jobs with rates determined on a linear function. For example, a job that is assessed to be worth ten points has a wage value ranging from $6,500 to $9,000. In contrast, a job that is assessed at 60 points has a wage range from $15,000 to $30,000.

The advantage to ranges is that workers can be rewarded periodically on the basis of seniority, tenure, or performance, without the necessity of advancement. Ranges also permit hiring or placement at different salary levels for the same position. This may be an important recruiting feature. Overlapping salaries between levels are also a possibility and again permit rewards for seniority, tenure, and performance. For example, in the situation illustrated in Figure 7.2, a worker at the 30-point level could be making as much as $17,500, whereas a new worker at the 40-point level might be earning as little as $11,000.

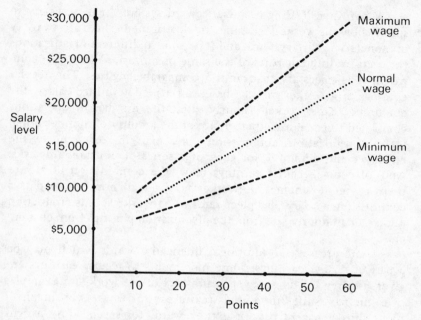

FIGURE 7.2. *Maximum and minimum wage rates for jobs at various point levels.*

The width of the range can vary or be the same at all points. The width is usually greater for those higher level jobs which reward managerial and executive positions (as in Figure 7.2). Consequently, an individual can be rewarded without promotion and receive the prestige or "implied significance" of salary increases. For example, consider a job that is assessed at 40 points. When the job structure and organization were developed, this job was determined to be one step in a career ladder in which a person would spend approximately five years. If at the end of the fifth year the organization does not want to advance the worker to the next position on the career ladder (assessed at 50 points), or the worker wishes to remain in his present position, or there are no openings at the next position, he can be rewarded with a higher salary within the range appropriate for the 40-point level.

Financial Reward Systems

Regular Earnings

When investigating financial reward systems, it is necessary to specify how the workers' earnings are determined. There are a variety of monetary reward systems, and if persons in different organizations (or even in different parts of the same organization) are to be compared, it is necessary to examine comparable figures. The regular earnings of a worker may be based on a predetermined salary, the amount of time worked (hourly rate), the number of operations completed (piece rate), a percentage of the amount of money earned for the organization (commission), or a figure agreed upon by the employer and employee for each of a series of nonstandard tasks. And, of course, regular earnings may be a combination of any of these payment schemes. A worker may get an hourly rate plus a commission, a salary plus piece rates when work exceeds production quotas, or an hourly rate from the organization plus tips from customers.

There are several additional financial rewards which may be a part of regular earnings. Some increments to regular earnings are given as a reward for some special aspect of the work—for example, overtime pay, shift differentials (extra pay for workers on inconvenient shifts), hazard pay, or extra rewards for special duty assignments (flight pay for Air Force pilots and additional salary for public school coaches). Other increments are for time not worked: holiday, vacation, and leave pay.

The importance of considering different kinds of regular earnings is that they may influence the results of empirical tests of theoretical statements in which "earnings" is a theoretical unit. If researchers use different empirical indicators to define the same theoretical unit of earnings, the research results may not be comparable. For the same reason, empirical studies concerned with individual perceptions of rewards may not be comparable.

Payments in Addition to Regular Earnings

Some organizations provide financial rewards in addition to regular earnings. Bonuses, for example, may be contingent upon such group or individual behavior as profit above a specified level, good attendance, or useful suggestions. The worker must recognize the contingent nature of a bonus if it is to have value as an incentive.

But the contingencies, if any, may not be obvious as in the case of Christmas or New Year bonuses; in this case the bonus may lose its incentive value and become an expected reward. Other financial rewards are possible. The organization can match a worker's contribution to savings plans or charities or have special plans for the acquisition of company stocks and bonds.

Payments in Lieu of Earnings

When work is not available for workers, some organizations continue to provide compensation. Industries with periodic layoffs may provide supplemental unemployment benefits or guarantee annual (or monthly) wages. Technological adjustment pay may be given to workers who have been displaced by changes in production methods. Many organizations have a severance pay policy for workers who are dismissed.

Financial Rewards for Special Occasions

Most modern organizations include in their reward program some fringe benefits which usually include a retirement program. Life insurance, accident and other medical coverage, and disability or early retirement programs also are offered.

This section gives some idea of the diversity of financial reward systems. Again, unless the empirical indicators are very specific and all possible influences are considered, the relationship of the theoretical unit of pay to other theoretical units may be ambiguous.

Nonfinancial Reward Systems

As if all the possibilities listed above did not make it difficult enough to determine just what rewards are provided to the worker by the organization, there are many worker benefits which are not financial in nature. Some of these benefits may be in the form of such personal services as housing service, financial and legal advisors and aid, medical services, and educational opportunities. Some organizations provide such recreational, social, and cultural opportunities as athletic leagues, special interest clubs, employee dances and picnics, and charter travel opportunities. Other nonfinancial benefits are related to the work situation: subsidies for the purchase and upkeep of work clothes and tools, transportation to the work place, the use of a company car, and eating facilities.

Benefit Preferences

Different workers prefer different rewards. Studies by Nealey (1963) and Nealey and Goodale (1967) demonstrate that differences do exist in benefit preferences and that these differences are systematically related to worker characteristics. After obtaining lists of rewards which had an equal cost to the organization, Nealey and Goodale asked workers to specify their relative desire for the rewards. Some of the rewards included in their studies were a $50 per month increase in pension benefits, a 6 percent raise, a 2½ hour reduction in the work week, hospital insurance, a union shop agreement, and an additional three-week vacation.

In demonstrating that such theoretical units as personal characteristics (age and marital status) are related to the theoretical units of reward choices, the researchers raise an important set of questions. What is the variety of rewards which persons want or expect from work? What influences these desires? What is the worker's priority for rewards? Do nondesired rewards have any influence on worker performance or attitude?

We agree with Lawler (1971) that organizations do not obtain maximal effectiveness from the rewards they provide because some of the rewards are not valued by workers. But how can this situation be avoided if nondesired or desired rewards vary from one worker to another? The *cafeteria reward system* (Nealey, 1963) would allot each worker a reward amount specified in dollar value, and each worker would determine how much he would receive in cash and how much he would receive in other financial reward alternatives.

For example, if a worker had $1,000 in benefits per month, he might decide to take $700 in salary, $50 in medical insurance, four Mondays off at a value of $120, $70 in a retirement plan, and a two-day extension to his vacation at a value of $60. Another worker may decide to use $750 in salary, $50 in retirement, $30 in a dental health plan, $50 in medical insurance, and a four-day extension of his vacation at a value of $120. The rewards in this example can be offered only if one individual's choices do not dictate another's. The major problem in administering this plan would be the bookkeeping involved in keeping track of individual reward choices. Computer administration of the system, however, makes this a feasible approach.

In considering work rewards, we must recognize that a worker's responses to rewards are based on such *perceptions* of those rewards as whether a reward is provided for performance, whether the person has ability to achieve a level of performance which will produce the desired rewards, whether the available rewards are desired, and whether the rewards and the performance required to achieve them are fair. Perception determines the worker's behavior. Expert consensus may be that a worker is receiving equitable pay for his job, but if the worker does not perceive that his pay is just, he will be dissatisfied.

The conditions under which a worker perceives his reward as just return for his performance have been investigated in several studies related to *equity theory* (Adams, 1963). Equity theory considers a worker's perceptions of his rewards to be a function of his perceptions of his own and others' input and output. *Input* is that which a worker contributes to performance: abilities; education; experience; effort; and so on. *Output* is that which he receives from the organization: financial and nonfinancial rewards; and other returns which derive from being part of an organization. The choice of "others" who are used for comparison will influence the comparison. The "others" may be members of the same work group, different work groups, similar work groups in different organizations, or friends.

The importance of the perception of rewards has been investigated by Zedeck and Smith (1968), who established a procedure for determining "just meaningful differences" in salaries. A "just meaningful difference" is the smallest salary change which alters the worker's perception of his salary. Is a $1,000 increase effectively the same as a $1,100 increase? If it isn't, will performance be influenced differently? Does a $1,000 increase mean the same thing to an individual who earns $7,000 a year as it does to one who earns $35,000 a year? Once the "just meaningful difference" is found, its relationship to job, salary, and supervisory level and personal characteristics should be investigated. Such information would aid in establishing meaningful wage ranges and understanding the desirability of promotions.

The realization of the importance of perception emphasizes the crucial relationship between the reward system and the operation of the organization. Workers should know the basis for their rewards and the relationship between performance and rewards. If a worker perceives no relationship between rewards and performance, he is not likely to improve (or even maintain) performance, even if, in fact, there is a contingent relationship.

Both objective and psychological variables must be considered when investigating reward systems, and the variables must be completely and unambiguously specified. Work rewards undoubtedly play an important role in determining worker responses to the job, but clear relationships will not be ascertained until all variables in the particular situation we wish to understand have been appropriately measured.

Summary

In this chapter we discussed how salaries are determined for various jobs and the importance of the perception of the salary. We also discussed the varieties of rewards organizations can provide to their members. Job evaluation provides a systematic determination of the worth of jobs to the organization. If the evaluation results are acceptable to management and labor, wage-related grievances should be reduced. Job evaluation also provides a framework for assigning salaries to new jobs.

Perceptions of work rewards can influence the worker's relationship to the organization. The perception of what the rewards are, their fairness, and their relationship to performance determine the effectiveness of pay as an incentive, and incentive contributes to a person's decision to join or remain with an organization.

References

Adams, J. S. Toward an understanding of inequity. *Journal of Abnormal and Social Psychology*, 1963, **67,** 422–436.

Belcher, D. W. *Wage and salary administration.* Englewood Cliffs, N. J.: Prentice-Hall, 1962.

Giles, B. A., & Barrett, G. V. Utility of merit increases. *Journal of Applied Psychology*, 1971, **55,** 103–109.

Lawler, E. E. *Pay and organizational effectiveness: A psychological view.* New York: McGraw-Hill, 1971.

Nealey, S. M. Pay and benefit preferences. *Industrial Relations,* 1963, **8,** 17–28.

Nealey, S. M., & Goodale, J. G. Worker preferences among time-off benefits and pay. *Journal of Applied Psychology,* 1967, **51,** 357–361.

Opsahl, R. L., & Dunnette, M. D. The role of financial compensation in industrial motivation. *Psychological Bulletin,* 1966, **66,** 94–118.

Zedeck, S., & Smith, P. C. A psychophysical determination of equitable payment: A methodological study. *Journal of Applied Psychology,* 1968, **52,** 343–347.

chapter eight

Attitudes and Motivation

Workers respond to many aspects of the work situation other than pay and rewards. Most worker responses can be classified as *attitudes*. Attitudes have been defined as affective responses (feelings), cognitive responses (beliefs), and behavioral predispositions toward stimulus objects. Sometimes one and sometimes another of these aspects of the theoretical unit of attitude have been incorporated into the empirical indicator for attitude measurement. But in this chapter we will utilize the most frequent definition—the affective aspect—in our discussion of attitudes toward such stimulus objects as work, the work environment, the work organization, co-workers, and so on. A worker's attitudinal responses or feelings about his job are often called *job satisfaction.*

Motivation has been defined as a predisposition to act in a specific way. The notion of motivation usually includes the concepts of both choice of behavior and amount of behavior. That is, motivation is concerned with "What does the person do?" and "To what degree does he do it?" Motivation, in a theoretical statement, is the *probability* that certain outcomes result from certain acts *and* the *value* or importance of these outcomes to the person doing the act.

Suppose two workers have an equal desire for high salaries which can be obtained through high production. One of these workers believes that it is *probable* that he can achieve the outcome of a high salary by working hard. The other worker does not believe (*low probability*) that he can achieve a high salary (*valued outcome*) by working hard. In this case, we expect the first worker to be more motivated to work hard. Or let us consider two workers who are equally convinced (*probability*) that hard work will lead to a promotion (*outcome*). The first worker values a promotion, whereas the second does not want to be promoted. The first worker is assumed to be more highly motivated to work hard.

Relationship between Attitudes and Performance

A great deal of research attempts to demonstrate a relationship between the theoretical units of job attitude and job performance. Vroom (1964) reviewed a large portion of this research literature and reported correlations between the two variables ranging from −.31 to .80 with a median of .14. A number of factors may account for such diverse results.

Job satisfaction has been conceptualized and operationalized in many ways. Many empirical indicators have been used for the theoretical unit of job satisfaction. Many investigators have created measurement devices according to a variety of attitudinal models to meet specific work situations or their own research requirements (Evans, 1969). There should be little surprise, then, that different measurement instruments, constructed to assess different conceptions of job attitudes, have produced a variety of results (Wanous & Lawler, 1972). Likewise, different measurement instruments constructed to assess similar conceptions of job attitudes have produced a variety of results. As we have emphasized, results can, and surely do, vary depending on the contextual situation in which the measurements are made. The relationship between job satisfaction and job performance may be quite different for assembly-line workers than for salesmen or shop foremen. It is possible that the relationship is negative in some situations and positive in others, and there are surely some situations where there is no direct relationship.

A further problem is the variety of performance measures (criteria). In Chapter Four we discussed several of the measures which have been and can be used to measure work behavior. There is no reason to believe that these measures are related to each other (Seashore, Indik, & Georgopoulos, 1960) or have similar relationships with such variables as job attitudes. If we evaluate a worker on five criteria measures (quality of work, quantity of work, absenteeism, ability to get along with coworkers, and conscientiousness), there may be no relationships between any of the criteria within a group—that is, quality may be unrelated to how much workers do, how often they are absent, and so on. These criteria also may have different relationships to any specific job attitude. A problem in previous research is the frequent use of only a single criterion. (We have pointed out some advantages to using more than one criterion.)

One performance measure to which attitudes can be related is *avoidance behavior*: absenteeism; turnover; requested transfer; and lateness. These are relatively objective measures. *Approach behaviors* indicate the degree of effort expended on the job and are studied indirectly by observing sales volume, production level, or performance quality, rather than the direction or intensity of workers' activities.

Most studies of the relationship between job performance and job attitudes have ignored individual differences. There has been a social science tendency toward general theories which explain the responses of *all* persons rather than toward theories which take into account diversity among persons. This is nowhere more true than in the realm of workers' interests in and expectations of their jobs. Research on worker satisfaction with various aspects of the job or the work environment may show low average satisfaction with pay. The organization may react by instituting a new salary policy which is applied to *all* organization members. In fact, however, it may be that only a portion of the workers were very dissatisfied with pay. The general strategy, then, has been to ignore the identification of subgroups in a worker population. A moderator approach might be a useful strategy to identify subgroups which differ in their job attitude-job performance relationships. Potential moderators might be found by investigating the relationships between satisfaction and performance for groups who differ in demographic, biographical, and personality variables, abilities, interests, and job characteristics.

Though many workers may respond favorably to jobs requiring personal involvement, responsibility, and autonomy, others may not (Hulin & Blood, 1968). Workers who are interested in advancement may be satisfied with their job and hard working because they see performance as a means of achieving promotion. Others on the same job may be very satisfied because they do not want advancement and recognize that by not working hard they can retain the same job without the additional responsibilities which accompany promotions. Both groups of workers are satisfied, but for very different reasons which would not be explored in the usual assessment of job satisfaction. Individual differences in the relationships between worker and job characteristics and worker attitudes are only beginning to be studied (Hackman & Lawler, 1971), but they deserve a great deal of attention if we are to give more than lip service to concern for individual workers.

Most empirical investigations of theoretical statements about the relationship between job satisfaction and job performance have implied a causal relationship. Most of these studies have been based on the notion that job satisfaction influences performance, but a few have suggested instead that the level of job performance influences job satisfaction. In both cases, however, only a few studies have assessed the variables in a sequential relationship so that a causal relationship could be discerned. That is, there would be an interval of time between the satisfaction measures (causes) and the criteria measures (effects), assuming this hypothetical causal direction. Instead, it has been frequent practice to simultaneously measure satisfaction and collect job performance criteria measures. Of course, such measures could be unrelated even if satisfaction has a strong causal influence. That influence would be found in the data only if the satisfaction measures were made *before* the performance period indexed by the criteria measures.

One technique which can be used to investigate the relative causal influences of theoretical units is *cross-lagged panel* analysis. In its simplest form, data are collected on two variables at two different times. For example, we might collect satisfaction and performance data for workers at one time. Six months later, we again collect satisfaction and performance data from the same group of workers. The correlation coefficient between satisfaction at time one and performance at time two is compared with the coefficient between performance at time one and satisfaction at time two. The correlation coefficients are related to the strength of causality. If the first of the coefficients is greater than the second we would assume that satisfaction causes performance to a greater degree than performance causes satisfaction. If both correlations are high we might assume that both influences operate simultaneously. (There are other possible interpretations of the coefficients; for a detailed presentation see Yee & Gage, 1968, and Sandell, 1971.)

Measurement Techniques

There are several procedures for assessing attitudes, but before choosing an approach, the researcher must consider the unidimensionality or multidimensionality of the attitude. Since jobs and work have many aspects, attitudes about jobs and work are multidimensional—that is, workers can have attitudes about each aspect (pay, coworkers, supervision, working conditions, opportunities for promotion). Furthermore, each of these job or work aspects can be treated as multidimensional. For instance, attitudes toward pay could involve attitudes toward regular salary, overtime, bonuses, and fringe benefits. Likewise, attitudes toward coworkers could involve attitudes toward immediate coworkers, subordinates, workers in other departments, and so on. Assessment of attitudes, therefore, should include as many aspects as possible of each of the work aspects. If we measure only one aspect of pay, we should not generalize to all possible aspects of pay. In other words, each *attitude measurement* should be unidimensional (pertain to a single specific aspect).

We could construct unidimensional attitude measurements by asking a single question for each aspect of the attitude object. One of our primary concerns in attitude measurement, however, is the reliability of the measurement. As previously indicated (Chapter Four), the more questions we ask about a specific aspect, the more reliable our measurement will be. Thus, we would ask several questions, each pertaining to the same attitude object.

Attitude Measurement

Researchers have several simple ways of obtaining information about job attitudes. For example, the *foremen's and/or supervisors' comments* on workers' attitudes can be analyzed on the assumption that foremen have considerable contact with workers and *should* be aware of their attitudes. This is often an unreliable and biased procedure, however, as the foremen's inferences and perceptions may be incorrect. Even if the foremen have an accurate perception of workers' attitudes, their comments may reflect primarily what they think the researchers or their superiors want to hear. Finally, and obviously, their comments may reflect their own attitudes. This is not a systematic analysis and it is impossible to compare different assessments made in this manner.

Likewise, the *grapevine*, or informal communication network, provides information about attitudes. The organization can become aware of problem areas as a result of information gathered from the grapevine, but here, too, there is the chance of distortion, falsification, and incompleteness.

In Chapter Five we discussed the problems of using *interviews* to obtain decision-making information. The problems of reliability and validity are similar when interviews are used to collect attitude information. But one interesting and useful interview function is the exit interview for which workers who are leaving the organization are requested to provide information about the company and their reasons for leaving. The value of the responses may be dependent, in part, on whether the termination is voluntary or involuntary. That is, information from someone who has been fired may be distorted by his feelings about being fired; information from a person who is leaving voluntarily may be distorted by attempts to justify his decision.

The authors are aware of one instance in which an exit interview was beneficially obtrusive. A company president, concerned about a high incidence of quitting and unaware of the reasons for it, instituted exit interviews. When employees were asked their reasons for leaving, it caused them to reconsider their job and work situation. Forced to think about the advantages and disadvantages of their jobs, many decided against leaving the company. (This is also an example of how tests, questions, and so on can affect behavior.)

Likert and Thurstone formats for scaled *questionnaires*, also discussed in Chapter Four, are appropriate for general attitude measurement. Here, however, we ask the respondent to tell us the intensity of his agreement or disagreement with attitudinal statements: "I would not exchange my job for any other"; "My job is fascinating"; "My job provides good chances for advancement." The Likert format requires a worker to choose from among five responses ("Strongly agree," "Agree," "Undecided," and so on). The Thurstone format might include similar statements, but the worker indicates only whether he agrees or disagrees.

Measurement of Motivation

One way to answer the question of why people work is to assess the meaning of work and what it can provide to the individual. We are concerned with individual desires, how they can be fulfilled in a work situation, and how much effort is expended to fulfill them. Researchers have identified many worker desires: security; esteem; self-actualization; prestige; recognition; autonomy; personal goods; and so on. To evaluate the strength of these desires, we can proceed in either of two directions. First, we can construct questions pertaining to the specific desires (or use an adjective check-list format) and ask workers to indicate the presence or absence of the desire in them. This procedure does not account for the influence of one desire on another, however. Second, we might assume a hierarchy of desires within an individual (Maslow, 1954)—that is, some desires are stronger than others, and an individual will seek fulfillment of his strongest desires first. If we measure the strength of desires we can compare groups and individuals with respect to differential fulfillment of desires.

To assess the fulfillment of desires we can ask two questions about each desire (Porter, 1961; Porter & Lawler, 1968). The first asks how much of the desired characteristic is now in the work situation. The second asks how much of the desired characteristic there should be in the work situation. Fulfillment of desires can be assessed by subtracting the response to the first question from the response to the second. The smaller the difference, the more the fulfillment of that desire in that work situation.

For example, suppose that the following questions were used to measure desire fulfillment for self-esteem and the responses are as circled:

The feeling of self-esteem a person gets from being in my position:

How much is there now?

minimum 1 2 ③ 4 5 6 7 maximum

How much should there be?

minimum 1 2 3 4 ⑤ 6 7 maximum

The difference (two) indicates some lack of fulfillment, and we would expect the worker to try to decrease the discrepancy. The proposition that there is a relationship between effort and measured discrepancies in desire fulfillment can be tested empirically.

The above analysis provides information with respect to the absolute level of desire strength within workers or it provides a comparison of desire strength among workers. Since motivation implies expenditure of energy or effort, we can measure motivation by obtaining estimates of effort. Guion and Landy (1972) obtained peer ratings on seven aspects of work motivation (professional identification [desire to continue self-development], team attitude, job curiosity, task concentration, independence/self-starter, persistence, and organizational identification). The higher the rating on such factors, the more effort expended and the greater the motivation.

Measurement of Job Satisfaction

Job satisfaction has been defined as the feelings about, or affective responses to, aspects of the work situation. Various formats can be used to measure job satisfaction—for example, checklists of adjectives or statements pertaining to the job. The procedure used by Smith, Kendall, and Hulin (1969) in their Job Descriptive Index includes a choice of *yes, no,* or *uncertain* in response to whether the statement or adjective is descriptive of the job. This technique does not ask the worker directly about his satisfaction with various job components but infers the level of satisfaction from the adjectives which the worker considers descriptive of his job. (This inference is based on empirical data collected during the development of the Job Descriptive Index.)

The difference score procedure described in the *Measurement of Motivation* section also can be used to measure job satisfaction. The difference between the responses to the "should be" and "is now" questions reflects satisfaction with the particular desire. This format can be used with other aspects of the job than those mentioned previously. For example, we might ask the two questions with respect to pay, working conditions, coworkers, or supervision. If "there is now" the same amount as there "should be," the worker is considered to be satisfied. If "there is" less than "there should be" of a job aspect, the worker is dissatisfied.

Difference scores should be interpreted with caution. An indication that "there is now" more than "there should be" has occasionally been interpreted as satisfaction greater than or equal to a zero difference. But careful consideration of the desire or job aspect under examination is necessary. If a worker indicates that he has more *pressure* in his job than there should be, this is obviously dissatisfaction. But if he indicates that he has more *responsibility* than there should be, it is not clear whether he is satisfied or dissatisfied, and it is therefore unclear how to interpret the difference.

Interpretation of the difference score likewise depends on the level of the responses to the two questions. Imparato (1972) has shown that a difference of 2, for example, reflects a different amount of dissatisfaction if 2 is the difference between 7 and 5 as opposed to 5 and 3.

Job satisfaction also can be assessed with the "Faces Scale" (Kunin, 1955) (Figure 8.1). Workers choose the face that expresses how they feel about a specific job aspect or the job in general. This essentially nonverbal scale is appropriate for many types of jobs and groups of workers.

FIGURE 8.1. *Faces scale.* (Adapted from Kunin, T. The construction of a new type of attitude measure. *Personnel Psychology*, 1955, **8,** 65–77. Reprinted by permission of the publisher.)

Validity

Regardless of the type of measurement or the aspects being measured, it is essential to establish the validity of the assessment instruments. We will assume that the measurement instruments have been shown to be reliable. The same methods are used for demonstrating reliability for attitude measurements as are used for performance evaluation measurements (Chapter Four).

Face validity establishes whether or not the instrument appears to measure the job aspect in which we are interested. It is often necessary to convince users of a measurement instrument that it assesses the concept it is intended to, and users are more likely to be convinced if the instrument has face validity. The final determination of whether an instrument has value, however, should be based on *content and construct* validities.

Content validity is the degree to which an instrument includes a representative sample of all relevant job aspects. If we are interested in satisfaction with pay, does the instrument measure satisfaction with salary, fringe benefits, incentive systems, and so on? If we are interested in satisfaction with the total job, can we measure satisfaction with pay, coworkers, supervisors, company policy, autonomy, work conditions and so on? Careful judgment determines which aspects should be included.

Construct validity is the degree to which we can successfully measure a theoretical construct and is determined by a combination of logical and empirical investigation. First, the investigator hypothesizes from his theoretical model of the construct (for example, work satisfaction) the relationships his measure should have with measures of similar and dissimilar constructs. Then he makes empirical tests of these hypotheses to determine if his measure furnishes the expected relationships. The formulation of expected relationships and empirical tests is a continuous process.

The multitrait-multimethod analysis (see Chapter Four) is one approach to construct validity. If we can demonstrate that several instruments measuring satisfaction with pay correlate with each other (convergent validity) and that each instrument reveals that satisfaction with pay is independent of satisfaction with supervision, coworkers, and so on (discriminant validity), we can *judge* that our satisfaction-with-pay instrument has construct validity.

The concepts of face, content, and construct validity indicate the degree to which we can assess satisfaction, desires, and motivation. But we are also concerned with the degree to which the instrument meaningfully distinguishes among individuals with varying levels of the measured characteristic. How well does the instrument distinguish between groups of workers that are supposed to be different on the measured characteristic? An *external groups criterion* examines a criterion that should be related to the variable measured by the instrument under investigation. For example, we could compare the average satisfaction scores of those who voluntarily leave and those who remain with an organization. If the averages are statistically significantly different, the instrument can distinguish between different groups. The problem, of course, is the choice of the criterion; the assumption is that the external criterion is a good measure of satisfaction. In this case, we assume that those workers who voluntarily leave an organization are less satisfied than those who remain, but, for many theoretical constructs, it is more difficult to find acceptable external criteria.

Another procedure for establishing validity is *triadic evaluation*, in which a potential item is responded to from three frames of reference (Smith et al., 1969). The worker responds with respect to his present job, the worst job he ever had or can imagine, and the best or ideal job. If he indicates that a particular aspect or item was liked or was descriptive of all three jobs, that item does not distinguish between the jobs and is not retained in the final instrument. Any item which does not distinguish between an employee's best and worst job and, by implication, differs for his present job, is also dropped. The items which are retained in the final instrument are those on which the present and *either* the worst or best job are evaluated the same. Items on which the present and ideal jobs are the same indicate satisfaction; items on which the present and worst jobs are the same indicate dissatisfaction. For example, if a worker indicated that "fair pay" was descriptive of his present and ideal jobs, but not descriptive of his worst job, then this item would be useful in a satisfaction measure.

Further Measurement Considerations

Several additional points should be made about measurement. First, is between- or within-person comparison an appropriate measurement model for motivation, desire fulfillment, and satisfaction? Between-person comparisons allow us to assess the variability of a group of workers on a particular job aspect. For example, we might assess satisfaction with pay for a group of workers and come to the following conclusion: Mike Moneybags is less satisfied with pay than Peter Plenty who, in turn, is less satisfied than Dizzy Honest. The interpretation leads the organization to adjust the salary of Mike Moneybags, but this does not change his satisfaction with pay. The reason could be that, relative to Mike's own desires, values, and so on, he is already satisfied with pay (but not as satisfied as other workers).

Within-person comparisons, on the other hand, indicate relative positions *within* a single worker with respect to several job aspects. In other words, the individual hierarchy of desires, values, and satisfactions is assessed. If we find that, relative to all other job aspects, Mike is dissatisfied with pay, the organization can take appropriate action. This type of analysis is consistent with the "cafeteria reward system" discussed in the previous chapter because it allows the worker to indicate his relative preference among various rewards (Blood, 1973). Comparison of an absolute level between individuals is not as relevant to attitudes, then, as it is to abilities. People respond to their work situation according to their personal hierarchy of work rewards.

The second point concerns the use of total job or *job-in-general* satisfaction scores instead of assessments of satisfaction with specific job aspects. What information is conveyed and what action can the organization institute as a result if only total scores are available? Very little. Again, two persons who have equal total satisfaction scores may require different considerations. Total scores do not indicate the relative value or pattern of satisfaction with specific job aspects.

Finally, if job attitude measurements are to be maximally effective, they should be made on a standard, periodic basis. A single, one-time job satisfaction survey can disrupt the very aspect being measured; regular surveys lessen the disruptive nature of measurement. It is difficult to interpret the information from a single survey because attitude assessment results gain meaning by comparison with previous surveys of the same or different groups. Repeated measurements provide natural comparisons. Attitude changes can be detected, and further investigations or appropriate changes can be made in response to negative changes. Regular surveys provide a useful gauge of worker sentiments, and they should be tailored to the characteristics, needs, and purposes of the organization.

Summary

We have discussed job attitudes, job satisfaction, and work motivation. We particularly emphasized methods for measuring these factors and validating the measurement instruments because we are dealing with such theoretical constructs as satisfaction with pay, self-esteem fulfillment, and desire for responsibility. One reason for assessing such constructs is so they can be used as one unit in a theoretical statement relating, for example, satisfaction with pay to performance. The major problem with such theoretical units is the development of reliable and valid empirical indicators. Finally, job attitude evaluations may be a step toward satisfying that valuable organizational resource, the worker.

References

Blood, M. R., Intergroup comparisons of intraperson differences: Rewards from the job. *Personnel Psychology*, 1973, **26,** 1–9.

Evans, M. G. Conceptual and operational problems in the measurement of various aspects of job satisfaction. *Journal of Applied Psychology*, 1969, **53**, 93–101.

Guion, R. M., & Landy, F. J. The meaning of work and the motivation to work. *Organizational Behavior and Human Performance*, 1972, **7**, 308–339.

Hackman, J. R., & Lawler, E. E., III. Employee reactions to job characteristics. *Journal of Applied Psychology*, 1971, **55**, 259–286.

Herzberg, F., Mausner, B., & Snyderman, B. *The motivation to work*. New York: Wiley, 1959.

Hulin, C. L., & Blood, M. R. Job enlargement, individual differences, and worker responses. *Psychological Bulletin*, 1968, **69**, 41–55.

Imparato, N. Relationship between Porter's need satisfaction questionnaire and the job descriptive index. *Journal of Applied Psychology*, 1972, **56**, 397–405.

Kunin, T. The construction of a new type of attitude measure. *Personnel Psychology*, 1955, **8**, 65–77.

Landy, F. J., & Guion, R. M. Development of scales for the measurement of work motivation. *Organizational Behavior and Human Performance*, 1970, **5**, 93–103.

Maslow, A. H. *Motivation and personality*. New York: Harper, 1954.

Mitchell, T. R., & Biglan, A. Instrumentality theories: Current uses in psychology. *Psychological Bulletin*, 1971, **76**, 432–454.

Porter, L. W. A study of perceived need satisfactions in bottom and middle management jobs. *Journal of Applied Psychology*, 1961, **45**, 1–11.

Porter, L. W., & Lawler, E. E., III. *Managerial attitudes and performance*. Homewood, Ill.: Irwin, 1968.

Sandell, R. G. Note on choosing between competing interpretations of cross-lagged panel correlations. *Psychological Bulletin*, 1971, **75**, 367–368.

Seashore, S. E., Indik, B. P., & Georgopoulos, B. S. Relationships among criteria of job performance. *Journal of Applied Psychology*, 1960, **44**, 195–202.

Smith, P. C., Kendall, L. M., & Hulin, C. L. *The measurement of satisfaction in work and retirement*. Chicago: Rand McNally, 1969.

Vroom, V. H. *Work and motivation*. New York: Wiley, 1964.

Wanous, J. P., & Lawler, E. E., III. Measurement and meaning of job satisfaction. *Journal of Applied Psychology*, 1972, **56**, 95–105.

Yee, A. H., & Gage, N. L. Techniques for estimating the source and direction of causal influence in panel data. *Psychological Bulletin*, 1968, **70**, 115–126.

Maintaining the Organization in the Future

The preceding chapters presented the problems that have arisen in work situations and discussed how researchers have attempted to solve them. The future will undoubtedly hold many changes from present patterns, and, therefore, the specific problems of concern to behavioral scientists will differ from the problems of today.

In this chapter we combine our crystal ball and the methods so far discussed and adapt both to an examination of what lies ahead for the organization. Future organizations will surely retain many of their present structural characteristics, but it is not very difficult to predict some of the changes and problems they will encounter.

The *modular* organization scheme, for example, is a recent and relatively untried innovation which substitutes self-contained groups or teams for the traditionally fixed and hierarchical units of the organization. These teams are composed of specialists who work together to solve problems, moving throughout the organization to those departments in need of their special skills. Such a team might consist of an engineer, an accountant, a personnel specialist, and an operations research specialist. They might be called upon to investigate a problem in scheduling and supplies in the production department. Upon completing their work on that problem they might undertake to facilitate the processing of orders in the marketing department. Both the positive and negative effects of modular structure need more study by behavioral scientists. We need to know what comparative studies may tell us about the advantages and limitations of both traditional and modular structures. The new model, however, may provide a degree of flexibility which will be helpful to large, complex organizations.

Other innovations may concern communications technology. Computers will be able to store and retrieve information much more quickly and efficiently than at present. This capacity should reduce the present need for many of the formal communications and reports which make their way through organizations. For example, salesmen's daily reports can be phoned directly into a computer system. Weekly and monthly reports could be retrieved from the system and compared to previously stored sales information.

More and more intraorganization communication will use computers and other communications equipment, decreasing the amount of face-to-face communication. For example, computer printouts of assessment and performance evaluation feedback can be relayed quickly to the worker. Communication innovations will be of interest to behavioral scientists as they will undoubtedly affect the theoretical units of attitudes and performance.

There will be increased participation in decision making by nonmanagerial workers. This trend is already evident in many segments of our society, and all indications are that it will continue in the near future. The demand for increased participation may be a societal phenomenon which will fade as values change, but it seems reasonable that the clamor for increased participation is an evolutionary, not a culminating, stage. In any case, behavioral scientists should examine the conditions which determine to what degree increased participation is beneficial and its effects on attitudes and production.

Although there will be different jobs and different work force characteristics, future job design problems probably will be similar to those of the present. One of the most helpful developments in job design would be the determination of general dimensions of job demands which could be specified in terms of human task abilities. If we were able to identify the abilities necessary to perform tasks, counseling for job choice could be greatly expanded and far more effective. It would also be possible to provide improved information about job opportunities to persons with the necessary skills but no idea of where they can be applied. Social scientists should expand and detail the task-ability system to cover many jobs and abilities and incorporate jobs which do not yet exist.

There will be changes, too, in the processes for obtaining organization members. Existing federal regulations and guidelines specify acceptable methods for validating tests, application blanks, and so on, but there is little specification of performance evaluation methods. Traditional performance evaluations are relatively subjective and therefore prone to unfair discriminatory bias. Future guidelines and regulations may indicate acceptable performance evaluation systems (perhaps along the lines of behavioral expectation scales).

More attention also will be paid to the content and construct validity of predictor tests. As was pointed out in Chapter Five, predictive and concurrent validations are difficult with the limited sample sizes of many organizations and because of other disadvantages. Most organizations may have to resort to job samples or other content valid tests as predictor information sources. But the effectiveness of synthetic validity should be examined more extensively as a possible alternative.

Organizations also may emphasize diagnostic testing rather than testing for screening. Applicants for positions at many levels would receive a battery of assessment instruments and subsequently be placed in jobs for which they are most suited *and* which make maximum use of talent in the organization. Better methods for evaluating training programs will be necessary as the emphasis on diagnostic testing calls for more training.

As employment demands and society's needs change, specialized workers will be unable to find employment. One solution may be such retraining programs as that recently sponsored by the federal government to orient unemployed aerospace engineers to the problems of municipal and state government operations. The premise of the program was that engineers could apply their knowledge and abilities to the problems of urbanization, pollution, and transportation. Likewise, some medical schools are admitting Ph.D's in chemistry, biology, physics, and related fields into two-year programs to train them as medical doctors. There is reason to believe that other classes of workers may be unemployable in the future. An examination of the effectiveness of retraining programs will be necessary to learn how well these persons perform in their new jobs and how retraining affects their personal values, goals, and life styles. The previously mentioned research on identification of job demands and task abilities also would facilitate the transfer of training inherent in such programs.

An area which has received very little attention from behavioral scientists but which should be of more concern in the future is labor-management relations. Behavioral scientists will be particularly concerned with the perceptions and interactions which are a factor in the speed with which labor disputes are settled. Stereotyped roles, communications processes, and the perceptions of arbitrators and negotiators are certainly influential, but behavioral scientists should study the conflicting pressures on the negotiator from constituents, other negotiators, arbitrators, and the general public.

Unions may wish to survey their members to determine the primary bargaining issues as both the composition of the work force (more women and minorities) and the work reward priorities change. The emphasis will be on personal growth and self-fulfillment rather than material objects, and personal growth obviously can be obtained from both leisure activities and one's job. This shift in emphasis will prevail for all job levels and, in fact, the blue-collar worker will receive increasing attention as the emphasis on education adds scores of blue-collar intellectuals to the work force. Here, again, job design research will have increasing value. Jobs must be designed to accommodate those who want more meaningful work or the freedom to derive meaning from leisure activities.

Four-day work weeks, guaranteed annual incomes, and early retirements are recent innovations. What are the effects of the four-day work week on the worker and his family? What kind of leisure activities will be sought and available? Will guaranteed incomes reduce the motivation to work or will they help retain members in the organization? What will those do who retire at the age of 45 after 20 years of service to one organization? Will they go back to school? Will they seek second careers?

These are only a sample of the questions which must be answered in the future. Behavioral scientists will be involved in the search for solutions and because *methods generalize relatively easier than results from situation to situation*, problem-solving procedures we have suggested throughout this book will almost certainly be applicable to both the problems we can foresee and those obscured by our focus on present realities and contingencies.

Epilogue

The topics and problems discussed here are divisible only in a book. They are intertwined in the actual operation of any organization. We chose one sequence for this presentation in this book—development of the organization, obtaining members for the organization, and maintaining the organization—but as was obvious when reading the theoretical statements, none of the individual problems is isolated. And although we ended our discussion with maintaining the organization, that is not the end of the problems. Consideration of the problems in maintaining the organization may influence the restructuring of the organization and redesign of jobs which in turn may influence the selection and training of members which in turn may influence the problems associated with maintaining the organization which in turn . . .

author index

subject index